ZALCO

GUSTAVO A. MADERO

VENUSTIANO CARRANZA

AUHTÉMOC

ITZTACALCO

ITZTAPALAPA

LOCAL Y FORÁNEO

TLAHUAC

XOCHIMILCO

GIRASOL

MILPA ALTA

THE
EATER
GUIDE TO
Mexico City

Edited by Nils Bernstein and Lesley Suter

Illustrations by Eliane Mancera

Abrams, New York

CONTENTS

INTRODUCTION

I couldn't tell you the best thing I ate in Mexico City. Over four glorious days, we had our fill of tacos, churros, guava pastries, mezcal, and more. We planned our trip carefully—getting reservations at the hottest tables was no easy feat for our large group—but so much of what we devoured was spontaneous and not documented for posterity. We simply happened to be in the right place at the right time, where a taquero caught our attention and we knew we needed to squeeze one more bite into the day.

This is the guide I wish existed then, one I would have pored over in the planning stages and marked up as I discovered new places and bookmarked favorites to share with others. It's one that takes Eater's unwavering commitment to spotlighting great restaurants and understanding the culinary DNA of a city, and peppers in what travelers should know to make the most out of every day (and of course, every meal).

That commitment began in 2005, with New York's complex dining scene providing ample fodder for us to document the changing landscape of food, culture, real estate, and more. Over time, Eater expanded its attention to Los Angeles, San Francisco, and Chicago, eventually growing the network to more than twenty cities, with guides and maps to countless international locations, including Mexico City. What started as a heatmap detailing the hottest places to eat evolved into a much deeper exploration, one worthy of a historic city with a staggering amount of culinary tradition and depth.

This book builds on our coverage of the Mexican capital, and aims to make sure that no matter where in the crowded city you are, you'll never be far from a stellar snack, drink, or Michelin-starred meal. Local expertise has always been core to Eater's mission, and our restaurant recommendations, guides, and storytelling come from those who know the ins and outs of a particular dining scene. For us, covering restaurants is much more than detailing menu items and prices, it's about global food trends, small businesses, consumer habits, and more. With our guidebooks, we aim to bring the same spirit to travel—not simply telling you where to eat, but why various foods are important, how immigration shaped the dining scene, and which restaurants have inspired generations of chefs.

For this book, we split the vast city into seven sections, from perennially popular Roma and Condesa to the Centro Histórico with its buildings dating back to the sixteenth century, to the far North, home to the most visited Catholic shrine in the world. In each chapter, we highlight the absolute best places to eat and shop, as compiled by our seven contributors, who have many decades of experience covering the destination. Digging in further, we explored the deeply rooted Japanese population in Mexico City and its influence on the culinary scene, as well as what to expect in a cantina, the neighborhood hub of social activity, where drinks are served with botanas (snacks) that encourage you to linger. We've detailed the best overnight trips to Tepoztlán, Oaxaca, and Valle de Bravo; hotels with particularly great restaurants to base your stay in; and even food tours for those who want even more of a guided trip.

There's something magical about Mexico City, a place where every street vendor has their own specialty, where restaurants stake their reputation on complexly flavored moles, and where the seafood is unbelievably fresh for a landlocked capital. There's no shortage of places to get your fill of "Vitamina T," as the locals call it—tacos, tamales, tlayudas, tostadas, tlacoyos, tetelas, and tortas—and then some. One thing's for sure: You'll be plotting your return before you know it.

—**Stephanie Wu**, editor in chief

PRO TIPS: In 2016, the city's official name changed from Distrito Federal (Federal District) to Ciudad de México (Mexico City), as a political move to give the city more independence from the federal government, akin to a separate state. As a result, the former nickname of "DF" is falling out of use, in favor of "CDMX." The latter is used often throughout this book. Neighborhoods are called colonias, and—unlike in the United States—are an integral part of postal addresses. Knowing the colonia you're in and where you're going is crucial to understanding and navigating the city.

In addition to this book, two things can help you navigate:
Eater's regularly updated map of the city and **our ongoing coverage of this special destination**.

EATER'S GUIDE TO MEXICO CITY

ESSENTIAL RESTAURANTS

Condesa
Doctores
Escandón
Roma Norte
Roma Sur
San Miguel Chapultepec

ROMA, C
& ENV

1

CONDESA
IRONS

ROMA, CONDESA & ENVIRONS

DINING

1. Bar El Sella
2. Cantina El Bosque
3. Cantón Mexicali
4. Caracol de Mar
5. Los Caramelos
6. Cariñito
7. Castacán
8. El Compita
9. Contramar
10. Las Costillas de la Condesa
11. La Docena
12. Gaba
13. La Hortaliza
14. Kura
15. Lina
16. Maizajo
17. Meroma
18. Mi Compa Chava
19. El Mirador de Chapultepec
20. Montejo
21. Páramo
22. Plonk
23. Rincón Tarasco
24. Rosetta
25. Sartoria
26. Taquería El Greco
27. Taquería Los Parados
28. El Tigre Silencioso

SHOPPING

1. Brutal
2. Delirio
3. Distrito Foods
4. Expendio Doméstico
5. El Grifo
6. Mercado de Medellín
7. Mercado el 100
8. Metate
9. Mis Mezcales
10. Vinos Chidos

CHAPULTEPEC

CONDESA

AVENIDA AMSTERDAM

AV. MICHOACAN

CIRCUITO INTERIOR

JUAN ESCUTIA

AV. TAMAULIPAS

AV. NUEVO LEÓN

SAN MIGUEL CHAPULTEPEC

ESCANDÓN

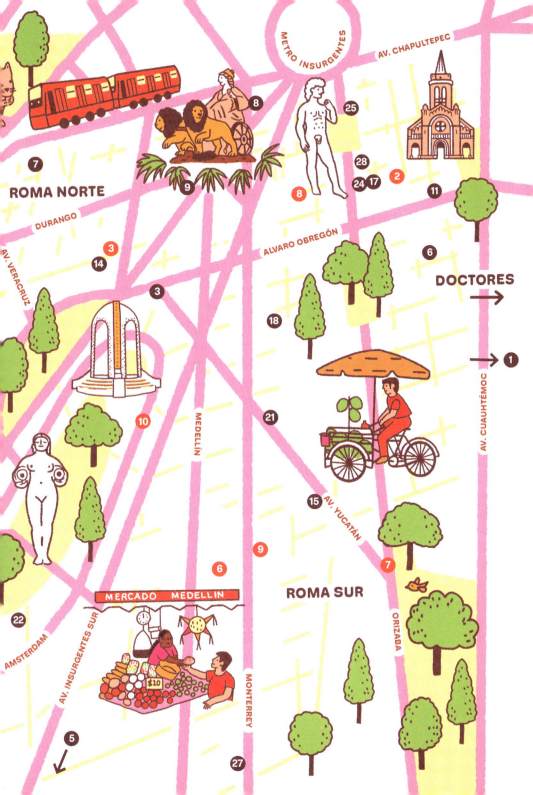

ROMA, CONDESA & ENVIRONS
DINING

Most people doing cursory research on Mexico City—where to stay, stroll, eat, and shop—will keep coming back to Roma and Condesa, the adjacent neighborhoods that are the heart of the city for most visitors. They're lovely, walkable areas that are centrally located and full of cultural and culinary attractions.

Condesa is usually referred to as "leafy," largely due to its two large parks (España and México) and elliptical, tree-lined Avenida Ámsterdam. Roma usually gets the moniker "bohemian" for no real known reason except perhaps people not wanting to say "hipster." Both are equally attractive and quietly chic, and while the borders sometimes blur, the diagonal main drag of Avenida Insurgentes more or less separates them. (Technically speaking, Condesa encompasses three colonias [neighborhoods]—Hipódromo Condesa, Hipódromo, and Condesa—but all are commonly referred to as Condesa, a format we follow here.)

Roma is quite large, and separated into Roma Norte (where most of the businesses are) and the quieter but emerging Roma Sur. Just east of Roma is colonia Doctores, a scrappy neighborhood that is nonetheless benefiting from its location as "Roma East." Shooting off Condesa to the southwest are the enclaves of Escandón and San Miguel Chapultepec, the former being a bit more working class, and the latter featuring many single-family homes, proximity to Chapultepec Park, and less of the tourist crowds that populate Roma and Condesa.

The area is architecturally beautiful as well, a mix of neocolonial, Beaux-Arts, belle époque, and art deco buildings, combined with considerable new construction that started in the wake of severe damage from the 1985 earthquake, and continued with its rampant gentrification over the last twenty years. That tension between old and new (and, more pointedly, the displacement of old businesses to attract wealthy locals, expats, and tourists) is especially evident in the dining scene. Many of the city's most acclaimed restaurants are here, but there is still a thriving street food and taquería scene as well, and the best way to explore these neighborhoods is to experience both.

1. Bar El Sella
Dr. Balmis 210,
colonia Doctores

Unlike most cantinas, where drinks take priority over food, the crowd at this Roma-adjacent favorite comes hungry for the chamorro (pork shank) that falls into shards with the merest nudge of a fork, Spanish chorizo (see page 55) braised in hard cider, and octopus bathed in smoked paprika and olive oil. Still, there are beers, Cuba libres, or pacharán—a Spanish digestivo—on most tables. Expect a wait during peak midafternoon lunch hours.

2. Cantina El Bosque
13 de Septiembre 29,
colonia San Miguel Chapultepec

Family gatherings and business meetings might be occurring elsewhere in this sprawling restaurant dating back to 1937, but most of the action is in the cantina section—just follow the noise and look for the gleaming bar. At most hours of the afternoon and evening (it closes most days by nine p.m.), there are rowdy tables of domino and dice games, or just groups of friends whiling away the day with cheesy potato quesadillas, tongue tacos, and milanesa manchega—a pounded beef or chicken cutlet covered in melted cheese and a rich guajillo chile sauce.

3. Cantón Mexicali

Avenida Álvaro Obregón 264, colonia Condesa

No Mexican city has as deep or long-standing Chinese roots as Mexicali, where Chinese laborers were brought in the 1910s and '20s to work the fertile valley and soon became land and business owners themselves. Cantón Mexicali is a cool take on that city's long-standing culinary mishmash, with dishes like chipotle shrimp with sesame and lime, and a chile relleno filled like a dumpling with a pork-and-ginger mix. The Dan Dan Noodles (shown below) stick to tradition, with mustard seeds atop the pickled mustard green garnish, but the star may been the green fried rice, packed with local veggies like favas, broccoli, quelites (wild greens), peas, and green beans. This is what culinary brotherhood is all about.

4. Caracol de Mar

Campeche 340, colonia Condea

From Grupo Contramar, under the capable direction of chef Mónica López Santiago, Caracol de Mar serves a seafood-focused menu of mostly small plates that's been a trademark of Contramar chef Gabriela Camara since 1998. More of a complement to Contramar than a clone, it stands out with dishes like mussel tamales and sea bass in the Yucatecan crab soup called chilpachole, and several vegetarian dishes as well.

5. Los Caramelos

Corner of Bajío & Chilpancingo, colonia Roma Sur

The tiny menu at this northern-style taco stand mostly revolves around what they call the caramelo—juicy long-cooked beef chuck, with or without cheese, in a flour tortilla with soft, fatty refried beans. Add your own garnishes to cut the richness: cabbage, habanero-pickled onions, a spicy peanut salsa. The stand opens at ten A.M. on weekends, making it a perfect pit stop when exploring the Saturday street market that runs along Bajío street, starting just east of Los Caramelos.

6. Cariñito

Calle Guanajuato 53, colonia Roma Norte

Roma and Condesa were pioneers of the Mexico City taquería as we now know it. In the 1950s and '60s, small taco stands and storefronts would open around the neighborhoods' many cinemas to serve moviegoers, becoming destinations unto themselves. Cariñito marks the ongoing evolution of the area's taquerías, a sweet, standing-room-only taco window with a Southeast Asian bent: slow-cooked pork, sticky eggplant confit, and long-cooked cauliflower with fermented beans, all seasoned with unconventional taco flavors like hoisin, tamarind, fried shallot, and piles of fresh herbs on housemade corn and flour tortillas.

7. Castacán

Puebla 387, colonia Roma Norte

The brilliance of Gabriela Cámara's other restaurant Contramar (page 13) is its simplicity, and it doesn't get much simpler than this colorful, retro-chic pork spot. It's devoted to the dual porcine jewels of Yucatecan cuisine, cochinita pibil (pit-cooked pork marinated in achiote and sour orange) and lechon al horno, roast pork with castacán, the word used in Yucatán for the crunchy-chewy chunks of pork belly.

flag after you flake the snowy-white fish. Finish with the fig tart and a carajillo. Even if this is your only meal, you can still tell people you did Mexico City right.

10. Las Costillas de la Condesa

Juan Escutia 104, colonia Condesa

Condesa still has some vestiges of the past. This spot has been known for its charcoal-grilled tacos since 1975. The signature smell of soot and corn and charcoal lets you know these are real tacos al carbón. The meats are always best campechanos (with added chorizo; see page 55), but vegetarians will be blown away by tacos and quesadillas made with various combinations of sweet corn, mushrooms, poblano chile, and cactus paddle.

11. La Docena

Avenida Álvaro Obregón 31, colonia Roma Norte

Seafood is the star at Tomás Bermudez's acclaimed restaurant (there's also a lively Polanco location): whole grilled fish, oysters raw and cooked myriad ways, giant clams, ceviche, and aguachiles (see page 53); the aguachile tatemado with shrimp and scallop is a must. But don't skip meatier options like hand-sliced jamón ibérico de bellota, chicharrón colombiano

Order your (hormone- and antibiotic-free) pork of choice as tacos or tortas, and choose from six house-made salsas on the table. Dessert? Tapioca pudding and ice pops.

8. El Compita

Corner of Puebla & Monterrey, colonia Roma Norte

The most iconic version of birria (chile-braised meat) hails from Guadalajara, where it's typically made with goat, never cheese, and served with corn tortillas on the side. But El Compita embraces Tijuana-style quesabirria—which took much of the rest of the world by storm before Mexico—made with beef and melted cheese and served with whole frijoles bayos (like a creamier pinto

bean) on the side. Try the volcán, a generous birria tostada with a cheesy crust.

9. Contramar

Durango 200, colonia Roma Norte

Everything you've heard about this institution from chef Gabriela Cámara is true. The seamless service is from another era, the sobremesa (page 29) can last for hours, and, of course, the dishes are among the most consistently stellar in the city. Order anything without fear, but first-timers should include the tuna tostadas, the scrambled eggs with potatoes and jamón serrano, and the whole snapper "Contramar," painted half with green salsa and half with red, to suggest the three colors of the Mexican (deep-fried pork belly), terrific hamburgers, and even real-deal Mexican-raised Wagyu steaks.

12. Gaba
Mazatlan 190,
colonia Condesa

Gaba chef Victor Toriz was born in East L.A. and raised in Mexico City, and worked at such scene-shifting restaurants as Bestia and Here's Looking At You in LA and Arca in Tulum. While not a Mexican restaurant per se, Gaba speaks to the city's cosmopolitan nature. Each dish nods to Mexico in some way, like giant ayocote beans with mussels, hibiscus with chicken paté, and chicken gizzards with esquites. Large-format dishes like whole fish and oversized pork tomahawk steak make it a terrific choice for larger groups.

13. La Hortaliza
José Vasconcelos 48,
colonia Condesa

The cheese-stuffed chile relleno taco in salsa roja may be the best vegetarian taco in a city with a surprising amount of vegetarian taco options. But most of owner and taquero Domingo Osorio's varying lineup of fillings are meaty and equally good, like bistec grilled with onion and potato, or chicharrón (pork rinds) in salsa verde. Located where several major arteries converge on the edge of Condesa, La

Hortaliza has charms that aren't readily apparent from its exterior (at least until you meet Domingo), but don't let that keep you from some of the best tacos you'll taste.

14. Kura
Colima 378-Local A,
colonia Roma Norte

The menu at this perpetually busy izakaya—izakaya being, essentially, a Japanese cantina (see page 138)—is enormous, but it's hard to go wrong; start with a salmon skin hand roll, pork fried rice, mapo ramen (ramen noodles in a spicy sauce of tofu, ground pork, and fermented black beans), interesting vegetarian rolls, and any of several tuna cuts served as sashimi or sushi. This is not the place for a quiet meal; come here instead for a boisterous time with friends over sake, Japanese beer, cocktails, and snacks. That said,

the lunchtime bento boxes are extremely generous and make a perfect solo meal at the bar.

15. Lina
Yucatán 147,
colonia Roma Norte

Chef Mariana Villegas worked at such iconic restaurants as Pujol and Contramar, with spells in New York and France, before opening the lovely Lina at the end of 2023. Vegetables and seafood are the focus, with innovative flavor combinations wielded with the confidence of a master painter: pickled mussels with parsnip and salsa verde; cauliflower with poblano chile, pistachio, mint, and a crisp chicken-skin garnish; and tartare of trout from nearby México state with rangpur lime, jicama, and hibiscus crème fraîche.

16. Maizajo

Fernando Montes de Oca 113, colonia Condesa

This tortillería, named after a rare strain of corn (máiz ajo, or garlic corn), started in 2016 as a tiny storefront where owner Santiago Muñoz studied and made tortillas from heirloom corn varieties at risk of extinction. Since then, it's been an influential force in educating locals about the myriad benefits of working with better-quality corn (he now supplies many of the city's best restaurants with masa). With the recent move to a converted house in Condesa, Maizajo has made the transition from workshop to full-fledged taquería and restaurant. Stop by for a quick snack at the streetside counter or a tipsy rooftop meal of antojitos (see page 53), or stock up on tortilla supplies for home.

17. Meroma

Colima 150, colonia Roma Norte

Chefs Mercedes Bernal and Rodney Cusic found instant success when Meroma opened in 2016, and it remains a favorite destination restaurant in Roma. It's more of a global than a Mexican restaurant, and yet the passion for local ingredients, as well as the chic design and charming service, makes it a natural fit for the city. Order a classic cocktail or a glass from the savvy wine list with some fried baby artichokes served over jocoque seco (akin to labneh) while you peruse the menu. Then try one of the many vegetable-forward dishes, maybe cauliflower with za'atar and green mole, or a half chicken with a zippy black bean purée and a pile of spicy local herbs, and end with a plate of regional cheeses. The menu changes frequently, so come often.

18. Mi Compa Chava

Zacatecas 172, colonia Roma Norte

More is more at this wildly popular seafood spot, which ostensibly is Sinaloa-style but offers combinations of ingredients that are entirely their own. The immaculate freshness of the seafood is what makes some of these wacky plates work so well, like the signature "Señora Torres," a teetering tower of layered yellowfin tuna, octopus, scallop, cooked and raw shrimp, red onion, cucumber, and avocado, with a bottle of chile morita salsa to douse at will. Or the tostada cachetona, of tiny calico scallops, crab, dorado ceviche, cooked and raw shrimp, and avocado, crowned with one giant sea scallop and dressed with a smoked soy-lime-chile sauce. To avoid the usual long wait, come when it opens at noon.

19. El Mirador de Chapultepec

Avenida Chapultepec 606, colonia San Miguel Chapultepec

El Mirador de Chapultepec has a friendly rivalry going with El Bosque (page 11) down the street (they have similar menus and atmospheres, with cantinas that are great for people watching), but either is a good pick for a hearty, boozy late lunch. Each has its fans: El Bosque's little livelier; El Mirador usually has more old-timers. Order tribilín—a kind of fish and shrimp ceviche with raw beef added—fish al pastor, and whole shrimp grilled with a chile and achiote marinade.

20. Montejo

Avenida Benjamín Franklin 261-A, colonia Condesa

There are a handful of great Yucatecan cantinas in the city—Xel-Ha and El Círculo del Sureste, just to name a couple—but Montejo is one with a distinct Mexico City edge. Here, the cochinita pibil (pit-roasted pork) is leaner than you'll get at roadside taquerías in Yucatán, the tortas (sandwiches) are huge, and there are chilanga (page 54) cantina classics like potato quesadillas, chamorro (pork shank), and whole grilled snapper. Also try the textbook versions of sopa de lima (Yucatecan lime soup) and tacos de escabeche de pavo (pickled turkey tacos).

21. Páramo

Avenida Yucatan 84, colonia Roma Norte

Páramo is several places in one: It's a bar for people who—like its owners—are past the age of deafening club music and going till dawn; it's a restaurant attached to a bar; it's an excellent taquería attached to a restaurant. The recipes mostly come from the owners' families and reek of comfort: meatballs in a tomato-chipotle broth and chamorro (pork shank) cooked carnitas-style in its own fat, as well as vegetarian plates like roasted poblano chiles with a mango and avocado sauce, and mushroom "carnitas" with eggplant purée and tomatillo vinaigrette. Most dishes can be ordered as individual tacos or as make-your-own-taco platters serving three to four people.

22. Plonk

Calle Iztaccíhuatl 52, colonia Condesa

Whether Plonk is a food-driven wine bar or a wine-focused restaurant is irrelevant; its flexibility is part of its charm. Come for a few glasses of minimal-intervention Old World wines from sommelier Romina Argüelles, or make a night of it with chef Flor Camorlinga's ingenious Mexican-Asian food (look for combinations like bone marrow with kimchi and Cotija cheese, or raw sea bass with serrano chile and matcha). Reservations recommended, due to its diminutive size and growing reputation.

23. Rincón Tarasco

Avenida José Martí 142 (entrance on Patriotismo), colonia Escandón

It's a losing battle to try to make carnitas at home as good as you'd get from a street vendor—especially one that cooks every part of the pig in copious amounts of its own fat. Much easier to go somewhere like Rincón Tarasco, which serves carnitas Michoacán-style (Michoacán is arguably the best state for carnitas, and "Tarasco" refers to a town there). As with most carnitas spots, you can order by the kilo to go ("maciza" is leaner meat, mostly shoulder; "surtida" is a bit of everything, including offal), but don't leave without trying the terrific bone-in taco de costilla, crisp-edged meat around a single pork rib running the length of a perfect tortilla.

24. Rosetta

Colima 166, colonia Roma Norte

At her flagship restaurant, which weaves through a warren of romantic rooms in a Porfirian mansion, Elena Reygadas established herself as one of Mexico's most recognized chefs, and for good reason. While it was initially labeled an Italian restaurant by people thrown by a pasta section on the menu, it's Mexican through and through. Within those pastas there might be tortelloni of hoja santa and smoked Oaxacan cheese, tagliolini with epazote and chile serrano, and huitlacoche gnocchi. Order liberally from the appetizers—maybe fermented carrots in white mole, tacos of romeritos (a briny green) and pistachio pipián (shown below), or a sweet corn and celery root tamal—then share some pastas and hearty mains.

25. Sartoria

Cerrada Orizaba 42, colonia Roma Norte

Modena-born chef Marco Carboni has created a mini Little Italy in this stretch just off Plaza Rio de Janeiro (the park with the replica of Michelangelo's David) with his flagship restaurant, Sartoria, the wine-and-provisions bar Bottega, and Pizzería della Madonna. All are highly recommended and have helped elevate the standard for Italian food in this city that was already crazy

28. El Tigre Silencioso
Colima 159,
Colonia Roma Norte

Chef David Hussong Castro's restaurant Fauna, located in the Baja California wine region of Valle de Guadalupe, is consistently voted one of the country's best, so it was no surprise that his stylish Mexico City cantina was a hit from day one. The wide-ranging menu skews northern—flour tortillas, giant clams, feather-light carne seca (dried beef), carne apache (a sort of Mexican steak tartare)—with an equally wide-ranging drink list of small-production wines, vermouths, craft beer, and signature cocktails.

for it (Italian is probably the second most popular foreign cuisine here after Japanese). Try his twenty-layer lasagna, or any mushroom dish during wild mushroom season from July to September.

26. Taquería El Greco
Campecho 440,
colonia Condesa

Even before the tacos, order the flan. It's both firm and yielding, giving in to the slightest pressure from your tongue, with a slight caramel flavor that's never cloying. Think of it as a sweet aperitif. Then, okay, order tacos. A gift from Middle Eastern immigrants, the tacos árabes (page 120), akin to doner kebab or gyros in that the meat is cooked on a trompo or rotating spit and served on thin pita-type bread, are not to be missed; the gringas come with cheese. Don't skip the beans with melted cheese, which have a charred aroma reminiscent of a campfire.

27. Taquería Los Parados
Monterrey 333,
colonia Roma Sur

It's true that the charcoal-grilled meat from Los Parados (which recently moved to this new location after almost fifty years in a storefront a few blocks away) has drawn some of the most loyal taco crowds since 1965; it's true that its trompo de arrachera (a rotating spit of skirt steak instead of the usual pork for al pastor) is one of the greatest ideas in the history of chilango cuisine; it's true that the salsas are without match; it's even true that the hamburger—which landed on the menu since the nineties—is something of a secret handshake among CDMX burger aficionados. Yet the pinnacle of this taquería is the taco of roast poblano chile strips with cheese, a deeply flavored, almost smoky taco that's delicious beyond description. Season with lots of chile morita salsa and lime.

17

ROMA, CONDESA & ENVIRONS
SHOPPING

Roma and Condesa are among the city's best walking neighborhoods, and you'll probably find more hot new shops within an hour of strolling than we recommend here. Generally speaking, both prices and quality are high across the board.

1. Brutal

Calle General Juan Cano 42, colonia San Miguel Chapultepec

There's no relation to the beloved Barcelona natural wine bar of the same name, but if you like the former, you'll love the latter. Wines here, including many not seen elsewhere in the city, are sold retail or to drink in-house for a modest corkage fee. Tasty small (and some large) plates come out of the open kitchen, and there's a well-chosen selection of tinned fish and other gourmet items available to go, for a picnic or late-night snack.

2. Delirio

Colima 114, colonia Roma Norte

You'll want to have Delirio on your radar as an all-day source for a pick-me-up, whether you are in need of an avocado toast in the morning, a duck carnitas torta in the afternoon, or a perfect macchiato at any hour. But keep it in mind for elegantly packaged house-made culinary souvenirs, like salsas, jams, sea salt, or marinated olives and onions.

3. Distrito Foods

Colima 365, colonia Roma Norte

Come here to buy artisanal mole sauces, salsas, jams, oils, coffee, liquors, and other Mexican pantry staples, plus some textiles

and dishware. They often have prepared foods and pastries for sale, especially around holidays, and can put together gift boxes for you.

4. Expendio Doméstico

Calle General Juan Cano 42, Colonia San Miguel Chapultepec

Next door to the wine bar Brutal is this high-end home goods shop, with items for the kitchen and dining table meticulously sourced from around the country. They will pack and even ship fragile items. There's also a location in posh Lomas de Chapultepec.

5. El Grifo

Juan Escutia 24 B, colonia Condesa

There's a huge selection of mezcal and Mexican craft beer in this tiny storefront. It hosts frequent tastings, but there are also a couple outdoor tables where

anything can be consumed on-site for no extra charge.

6. Mercado de Medellín

Campeche 101, colonia Roma Sur

One of the city's best covered neighborhood markets, Medellín (its official name is Mercado Melchor Ocampo, but everyone calls it by the street that runs along its west side) has more than five hundred vendors but is best known for its selection of products from Central and South America as well as Cuba (some think it's called Medellín for the large number of Colombian vendors). It's a good spot to find less-common fruits, vegetables, and chiles. The market had primarily Jewish Mexican vendors and management until the mid-eighties, when the 1985 earthquake spurred much of colonia Roma's Jewish population to leave the damage-prone area.

7. Mercado El 100
Corner of Antonia M. Anza & Orizaba and Coahuila, colonia Roma Sur

This all-organic Sunday farmers' market has a prerequisite that all products from its fifty-some vendors are grown or produced within one hundred miles of Mexico City—hence the name. Look for rabbit and river trout, tomatoes that range in size from marble to volleyball, medicinal herbs, monofloral honey, vegan tamales, and much, much more.

8. Metate
Durango 280, Colima 208, and Orizaba 92, colonia Roma Norte

This is the spot for handmade home goods, mostly for your kitchen and dining rooms. It's especially good for candles and candle holders, and barro vidriado (pottery with a glassy glaze) from Michoacán state.

9. Mis Mezcales
Coahuila 138, colonia Roma Sur

The mezcal selection at this tiny shop is probably the city's best, not just for its overall variety but for the small brands that can be near impossible to find outside this store. There's also Mexican rum, gin, and whiskey, and mezcal paraphernalia like T-shirts, books, flavored salts, and jícaras, the hollowed and dried gourds traditionally used for imbibing. Consider booking an enlightening private tasting in their upstairs gallery, and follow their socials for frequent in-house events.

10. Vinos Chidos
Avenida Ámsterdam 297, colonia Condesa

Noah Tavares started this natural wine shop (now with several locations in addition to this flagship) as a delivery service during the pandemic and now has several stores that are at the cutting edge of Mexico City's fast-growing wine scene. There are frequent in-store tastings, plus weekly events for club members (worth joining for wine people staying in town awhile). You're unlikely to see these wines in other stores; many are exclusive to Vinos Chidos.

BEYOND RESTAURANTS

Coffee Shops
Q'Pedro Pablo
Cardinal Casa de Café
Cumbé
Dosis
El Ilusionista
Qūentin

Bars
Baltra
Brujas
Casa Prunes
La Clandestina
Hiya
Natas
Niv
El Palenquito
Rayo
Selva
Si Mon Vinos
    Mexicanos
Tlecan
Yeccan Cervecería

Bakeries
Bakers
Ficelle
La Otilia Gluten-Free
Panadería Rosetta
Pancracia
Patisserie Dominique
Saint

Sweets
Dichoso Cacao
Helados Cometa
Nevería Roxy
Oscuro Puro
Tout Chocolat

A BRIEF HISTORY OF DINING IN MEXICO CITY

By Raquel del Castillo García

The cuisine of Mexico City is both a time machine and a Tower of Babel. There are ingredients, techniques, and dishes around today that remain virtually unchanged since centuries before the arrival of the Spanish in 1519. At the same time, Mexico City restaurants, street stands, and markets are a thrilling tangle of deep-rooted influences from Europe, Asia, Africa, the Americas, and the Middle East, as well as every part of Mexico itself.

Mexico, in turn, has fed the world with its native ingredients like corn, beans, tomatoes, squash, chiles, avocados, agave, vanilla, and chocolate. These formed the anchor of a prehispanic diet that was sufficiently nutritious despite a lack of dairy animals and cooking oils. Much of this nutrition was due to nixtamalization, the millennia-old process of soaking corn in a slaked lime solution, which loosens the hulls and softens the kernels enough so they can be ground into a dough. Besides improving taste and workability, the process makes its nutrients bioavailable—specifically tryptophan, the precursor to niacin—thus preventing fatal epidemics like pellagra.

The tortilla is the base of the Mexican food pyramid, and the Mexico City diet revolves around what locals call "Vitamina T": tacos, tamales, tostadas, tlacoyos, tlayudas, tetelas, and tortas (the latter a sandwich made with bread, not tortillas but an honorary member of the T club in CDMX). However, this valorization of corn and its Indigenous roots is a relatively recent phenomenon in Mexico City, the part of the country where political, social, economic, and migratory forces have collided for centuries.

Before the Spanish conquests, Tenochtitlan (today the Centro Histórico and environs) was the center of the Aztec Empire and one of the biggest cities in the world, with at least two hundred thousand people. Upon arriving in November 1519, Spanish conquistador Hernán Cortés and his men were amazed by the quantity and quality of food and drink in the busy markets. In a letter to the king, he wrote:

One square in particular is twice as big as that of Salamanca and completely surrounded by arcades where there are daily more than sixty thousand folk buying and selling . . . There is a street of game where they sell all manner of birds that are to be found in their country, including hens [turkeys], partridges, quails, wild duck, fly-catchers, widgeon, turtle doves, pigeons, little birds in round nests made of grass, parrots, owls, eagles, vulcans, sparrow-hawks, and kestrels . . . They also sell rabbits, hares, deer and small dogs which they breed especially for eating . . . There is a street of herb-sellers where there are all manner of roots and medicinal plants that are found in the land . . . All kinds of vegetables may be found there, in particular onions, leeks, garlic, cress, watercress, borage, sorrel, artichokes, and golden thistles.

There are many different sorts of fruits including cherries and plums very similar to those found in Spain. They sell honey obtained from bees, as also the honeycomb and that obtained from maize plants which are as sweet as sugar canes; they also obtain honey from plants which are known both here and in other parts as maguey, which is preferable to grape juice; from maguey in addition they make both sugar and a kind of wine, which are sold in their markets . . . Maize is sold both as grain and in the form of bread and is vastly superior both in the size of the ear and in taste to that of all the other islands or the mainland. Game and fish pies may be seen on sale, and there are large quantities

of fresh and saltwater fish both in their natural state and cooked ready for eating.
—from *Five Letters of Cortés to the Emperor: 1519–1526* (W. W. Norton & Company), translated by J. Bayard Morris.

Cortés spoke of the feasts of Moctezuma II, ruler of Tenochtitlan, with more than a thousand noblemen and servants eating countless dishes served by hundreds of waiters, with Moctezuma himself serving some thirty dishes and drinking from several jugs of prepared cacao ("a fruit resembling our almonds, which they sell crushed," according to Cortés) with different savory seasonings.

With the fall of Tenochtitlan and establishment of Mexico City as the capital of New Spain, a hybrid cuisine developed. Spain introduced chickens, pigs, and cows (and with that, cheese and cream), while the new populace accommodated staples like corn, beans, tomatoes, squash, chiles, and other native fruits and vegetables. Still, political and class issues complicated any clear definitions of "Mexican cuisine," especially as it was practiced in the capital city.

It's no coincidence that every September 15, Mexicans eat pozole—a prehispanic hominy stew—to celebrate Mexico's independence from Spain in 1810. Yet anthropologist José Luis Juárez López points out that pozole wasn't popularized as a patriotic dish until the 1960s, when ingredients like oregano, lime, chile, radish, and lettuce were added to represent the red-white-green of the Mexican flag, but also to move it away from its origins as just hominy (nixtamalized corn kernels) and water.

Indeed, the post-Independence search for national identity—culinary and otherwise—was complicated throughout the 1800s by Indigenous insurgencies and civil wars, the loss of northern Mexico (from California to Texas), the French invasion in the 1860s, and the dictatorship of Porfirio Díaz, which started in 1876. Díaz brought prosperity for a time, but also classism and corruption, and a general disdain for Indigenous culture while lionizing everything French, including food.

High-society tables in late-nine-teenth-century Mexico City were laden with escargot, Champagne, and crème brûlée. As cafés and restaurants emerged, they had French and French-inspired food and design. At public establishments, "Mexican" food was mostly found in the handful of early cantinas (see page 138); even tacos weren't commonly called "tacos" until the twentieth century (see page 114), despite people long having eaten food inside tortillas.

The first two decades of the twentieth century—the tail end of Díaz's reign and the decade-long Mexican Revolution—were synonymous with hunger, looting, and armed conflicts for the majority of the population. Since this was a period of scarcity, most of the population returned to eating from the milpa, the Indigenous system of regenerative agriculture that had historically been used to grow the country's key crops. The dishes cooked were far from the status-driven food that had been in vogue: simple tacos, beans, greens, rice in tomato broth, stewed wild animals, and basic moles. Humble though wartime cooking and subsistence farming were, they started a reappreciation for Mexico's native foods, along with increased awareness of the myriad regional cuisines in the huge and diverse country, and so began a slow reassessment of what "Mexican cuisine" meant.

Mexico City's population roughly tripled every twenty years from 1910 to 1970. With this stratospheric growth came an influx of eating establishments, though the wide class divide meant that most commuting workers ate in markets, casual cantinas, or homey fondas, while elites ate in upscale cantinas and restaurants that were still geared toward European cuisines, primarily French, Spanish, and German.

Street food has existed since prehispanic times, when simple things like atole (corn gruel) and tamales were sold by market vendors in tianguises (outdoor markets). The urban population boom brought more street food options, though the middle classes would mimic these dishes at home, to avoid real or perceived hygiene issues on the streets. Recipe books in the 1900s started including recipes for things like sopes, chalupas, tacos, and tlacoyos alongside elaborate Spanish and French dishes. Relatively recent inventions, like the torta (credited to Tortas Armando in 1892) and huaraches (fried masa topped with beans; see page 42), said to be invented in the stands around

Mercado Jamaica in the 1930s, are, of course, still popular today.

Yet proper restaurants were a different beast altogether. Until the 1990s, eating in a restaurant in Mexico City meant you were celebrating, wealthy, or both. In the seventies and eighties, people went to eat "gourmet" food at places like Bellinghausen, Focolare, Champs Elysées, and Delmonico's in colonia Juárez's Zona Rosa, then a center for art, culture, and intellectual debate. This see-and-be-seen culinary scene moved in the nineties to Polanco, where you might still hear people rhapsodizing about lost gems like Le Cirque, Ciboulette, L'Olivier, and L'Alsace. The idea of eating Mexican food in a "nice" restaurant is, for the most part, a relatively recent phenomenon.

In the late twentieth century, a handful of Mexico City chefs stopped looking to Europe for inspiration, instead researching their own culinary traditions and presenting them with global savvy, becoming legends in the process.

Alicia Gironella started a culinary institute in 1980, and in 1993 she opened El Tajín with her husband, Giorgio De'Angeli. Her vision of Mexican food was a kind of Indigenous avant-garde, with then-radical white and pink moles, and her Avándaro salad of squash blossoms, quail eggs, and toasted amaranth. Patricia Quintana published her first book of Mexican cuisine in 1975, and her 1986 book *The Taste of Mexico* made waves internationally. She's also credited with inventing the jicama taco—with jicama as the tortilla—at her restaurant Izote, where she filled it with avocado or chipotle crab.

Mónica Patiño began to infuse traditional Mexican cuisine with French techniques and Asian flavors. The restaurants that brought her fame, MP Café Bistro and Náo, are no longer around, but her Casa Virginia winks to her past with dishes like avocado tostadas draped with jamón ibérico and a ginger-infused sauce. The now-classic Contramar (page 13) was considered radical when it opened in 1998, with chef-owner Gabriela Cámara putting Pacific coast seafood-shack dishes in a fine-dining context.

Though their individual cooking styles vary enormously, these and many other chefs' insistence on placing Mexican food on a par with the world's finest cuisines has had an immense impact on the current generation of chefs, educating the world about food beyond Mexican

American and Tex-Mex, and ultimately garnering international media attention and establishing Mexico City as a culinary destination. In 2010, Mexican cuisine was declared a Cultural and Intangible Heritage of Humanity by UNESCO. Today, it's finally easier to find a Mexican restaurant in Mexico City than a foreign one.

Casual venues like taquerías (page 43), puestos (page 43) and fondas (page 56) are in fashion for several reasons, among them nostalgia, finances, fancy-restaurant fatigue, and wanting to consume locally, both in terms of ingredients and eating within our neighborhoods and communities. Many of the old-fashioned, home-style dishes at cantinas and on comida corrida (page 122) menus can feel fresh to people accustomed to eating more globally at home and in restaurants.

At the same time, the post-pandemic influx of so-called digital nomads and other immigrants from the United States, Canada, and Europe has restaurant owners raising prices and adjusting menus to cater to this relatively flush new clientele, while many longtime residents and businesses are driven out by the processes of gentrification. Just as beloved NYC staples like cheap diner breakfasts and deli sandwiches are ever rarer in parts of Manhattan, it's harder to find simple, traditional, affordable options in central Mexico City neighborhoods like Roma, Condesa, and Juárez, even as they have become feted as global dining destinations.

Still, the city's parade of fine-dining restaurants with tasting menus and "world's best" honors are leaning into the ingredients and techniques that form Mexico City's culinary core. At Pujol (page 86), Enrique Olvera put his years-aged Mole Madre on a plate by itself, with no protein, to highlight its grandeur. Elena Reygadas's sophisticated tamales and herb-driven desserts at Rosetta (page 16) are steeped in tradition. Jorge Vallejo's Quintonil (page 86) is named for humble amaranth greens, and he applies the nixtamalization process to other fruits and vegetables. It's a cuisine in constant evolution but whose roots keep reaching deeper.

DINING ETIQUETTE AND TIPS

Whether at a taco stand or a formal restaurant, politeness rules in Mexico City. Even if you're not a Spanish speaker, be a champ and try to at least break out your "buenas tardes," "por favor," and "gracias." Here's a handful of other tips to keep things running smoothly.

Attire

There is still a level of respectful formality expected in a restaurant environment. In terms of dress, even at casual spots, you're smart to avoid sleeveless tops, open-toed shoes, and shorts. In terms of comfort, remember that Mexico City is fairly high (7,350 feet altitude), so it never gets extremely hot, and cools down considerably at night.

Cash

It's always good to have cash on hand, especially larger coins and smaller bills. Most street stands don't accept credit cards and often don't have change for large bills. Coins can be handy for public bathrooms (usually five or six pesos), street musicians, tipping the people who bag groceries, and a myriad of other uses.

La comida

Remember that the main meal of the day is la comida, a late lunch, generally around two to five P.M. While the influx of tourism has led most restaurants in touristy neighborhoods to adjust hours to accommodate US preferences, be sure to check restaurant hours if you're looking for a noon lunch or an early-bird dinner. Typically, breakfast times are similar to the United States, but many people will grab a snack around eleven or noon to tide them over until la comida. Unlike in many European countries, the long, late dinner is more of a celebratory than an everyday (or even every week) thing; since "lunch" often goes until late afternoon or even early evening, "dinner" might just be tacos, or snacks with drinks. One important difference from the US is that lunch and dinner menus are almost always the same. Many taquerías are open late to accommodate late-night revelers.

La cuenta

Waiters will almost never bring the check without being asked. When you want it, catch their eye and either say "La cuenta, por favor" or make the seemingly universal "signing a check in the air" motion with your hand.

Eat with your hands

No utensils? No problem. Even in a fine-dining environment, antojitos—tacos, tostadas, sopes, gorditas, tlacoyos, tetelas, and the like—are generally eaten with your hands. Similarly, if tortillas are presented with a dish, using them as an eating implement is expected.

Getting around

When exploring within central neighborhoods, walking is often the best bet, especially considering the city's notorious traffic. Otherwise rideshare companies like Uber, DiDi, and inDrive are almost never more than ten minutes away at any hour. The subway and Metrobus (an aboveground mass-transit system) can be useful for traveling long distances, and there's also a bike share system called Ecobici. Check travel times if going to or from Polanco, Coyoacán, or the Centro Histórico, as traffic and sudden street closures can turn what should be a fifteen-minute trip into an hour.

Limón y salsa

While in some countries adding salt or pepper can be seen as an affront to the chef, adding seasoning in the form of lime and/or salsa to a dish in Mexico is fully accepted, even encouraged, as evidenced by their ubiquity on restaurant tables and taquería counters. In general, very few dishes are extremely spicy when they arrive at the table (except for most aguachiles; page 53); rather, you're expected to add heat to taste.

Meat doneness

Specifying meat doneness can feel like a moving target in CDMX, largely because meat is usually thin-cut and thus not thick enough to warrant such specifying. To complicate things further, thick steaks are often found in Argentinian restaurants, where the terminology can differ. When in doubt, feel free to specify your preferred doneness in English, as the server will likely know how to convey this to the kitchen. But roughly speaking, in most places they'll understand "rojo" to be rare, "medio rojo" for medium-rare, "medio" for medium, "tres cuartos" for medium-well, and "bien cocido" for well-done. In an Argentinian steakhouse, they may favor "muy jugoso" (rare), "jugoso" (medium-rare), "al punto" (medium), "cocido" (medium-well), and "bien cocido" (well-done). At most Mexican and Argentinian establishments, medium is generally considered to be the ideal temp and will be the default if you don't specify.

Provecho

When passing through a restaurant and either locking eyes with, or squeezing uncomfortably past, another table, smile and nod and say "Provecho" (short for "Buen provecho," meaning "Bon appétit"). When someone does the same to you, smile and nod.

Reservations

As in most cities, reservations are recommended for especially popular, or more formal, restaurants. Services like Tock, Resy, and OpenTable are in use throughout Mexico City, and generally speaking, if reservations are likely to be needed, the restaurants' own websites will have links or instructions on how to do so online or by phone. Some restaurants that typically require reserving far in advance are Contramar (page 13), Masala y Maíz (page 36), Nicos (page 151), Pujol (page 86), Quintonil (page 86), and Rosetta (page 16).

Sobremesa

Sobremesa (see also page 56) is the tradition of lingering over drinks, and sometimes more food, even after dessert. Don't feel bad about doing so, as long as you're consistently ordering something. People have been known to sobremesa long enough to order a full second meal.

Straight up

Tequila and mezcal are typically served straight up (say "derecho" or "solo"). The concept of the chilled shot, or even on the rocks—let alone "muddled with four lime wedges" and the like—isn't common and might take more explaining than you think.

Tipping

At restaurants, a 15 percent tip is considered both generous and standard. At counter service places (street stands, coffee shops, bakeries, etc.) there is usually a tip jar, much like in the United States. With credit cards, tips are charged with the card, rather than written on the receipt, and the transaction is done at the table so that your card doesn't leave your sight. When they run your card, say the percentage amount—such as "con quince" with 15 percent)—that you'd like to add.

Centro
Guerrero
Merced Balbuena
Morelos
Tepito

HISTÓ C

2

ENTRO
RICO

CENTRO HISTÓRICO

DINING

1. Azul Histórico
2. El Cardenal
3. Casino Español de México
4. Churrería El Moro
5. Finca Don Porfirio
6. El Gallo de Oro
7. Lady Tacos de Canasta
8. Limosneros
9. Masala y Maíz
10. Migas La Güera
11. Migas Mary
12. Paxia
13. El Pozole de Moctezuma
14. Quesadillas Cuba
15. Ricos Tacos Toluca
16. Salón Familiar La Mascota
17. Tacos de Canasta El Flaco
18. Tacos El Puma
19. Taquería Coco-Loco
20. Taquería El Torito
21. Tezontle
22. Tripolandia

SHOPPING

1. Mercado de Artesanías La Ciudadela
2. Mercado de la Merced
3. Mercado San Juan E. Pugibet
4. Mercado Sonora
5. Tianguis La Lagunilla

GUERRERO

BALDERAS

AV. D. R

TEPITO

MORELOS →

AV. P. DE LA REFORMA

CENTRO

EJE CENTRAL

AV. CHAPULTEPEC

LOZA

MERCED BALBUENA

CENTRO HISTÓRICO
DINING

The Centro Histórico is, per its name, the oldest part of Mexico City and the region's political, spiritual, and socioeconomic core since before the Spanish conquest of Tenochtitlan. The neighborhood boasts breathtaking gothic, baroque, and neoclassical marvels that radiate in every direction from Plaza de la Constitución (aka Zócalo), the largest public square in Latin America. Roughly fifteen hundred buildings in the Centro, built between the sixteenth and twentieth centuries, are officially designated as being of historical or architectural importance. As you might expect, many of the city's most important sights are here.

The Centro Histórico went through a period of restoration and rejuvenation after the 1985 earthquake, and again in the early 2000s with efforts to draw younger residents. Though it's still far from a "hot" area (which is much of its appeal, honestly), it warrants more than an afternoon of obligatory sightseeing. To that end, several boutique hotels have opened here recently, luring top chefs to open new restaurants in colonial edifices. It makes for a terrific mix of old and new, high and low, that is a microcosm of everything great about eating and drinking in the city.

1. Azul Histórico
Isabel La Católica 30,
colonia Centro

Since opening Oro y Azul at UNAM in 2000, cookbook author, culinary investigator, and mentor chef Ricardo Muñoz Zurita—who literally wrote the encyclopedic dictionary on Mexican gastronomy (*Diccionario Enciclopédico de la Gastronomía Mexicana*)—has cultivated a lovely space set in the courtyard of a charming colonial palace under a canopy of treetops. The location is ideal for quick bites such as regional guacamoles, tacos de lechón, or the house sopa de tortilla (tortilla soup), as well as more leisurely meals centered around the chef's textbook moles or the monthly special menus that highlight different regions of Mexico.

2. El Cardenal
Palma 23,
colonia Centro

Since 1969, the quintessential spot for Mexican breakfasts is this original location of El Cardenal, a monument to regional Mexican gastronomy. Try huevos aporreados, a saucy dish of eggs and dried beef, or ahogados en frijoles de la olla, flavorful whole beans with eggs poached in the broth. Even simple entrées like tangy red enchiladas mineras from Hidalgo or a show-stopping chamorro pibil (pit roasted pork shank) are Mexican haute cuisine at a level worth appreciating. Plan for a long wait during weekend breakfasts.

3. Casino Español de México
Isabel La Católica 29,
colonia Centro

Casino Español was born in 1863, envisioned as the finest Spanish social club in the Americas. It was housed in several Centro locations before the city's Spanish elite commissioned architect Emilio González del Campo to build this palace, which opened in 1905. The building is an eclectic and over-the-top marvel of neorenaissance and neobaroque architecture, with some Arabic touches and museum-quality art, furniture, and stained glass. Admire the room and order Spanish classics like callos a la madrileña (stewed tripe), fabada asturiana (white beans and sausage), and a beef filet grilled tableside on a hot stone.

4. Churrería El Moro
Eje Central Lázaro Cárdenas 42,
colonia Centro

There's nothing more romantic than sharing an order of slender churros and cups of Mexican hot chocolate at the original location of Churrería El Moro, one of the city's most celebrated institutions since 1935. They're a sweet break from an antojitos crawl in Centro Histórico, complete with a show as you watch endless churro spirals being fried fresh in the space that is synonymous with churros in Mexico City.

5. Finca Don Porfirio
Avenida Juárez 14,
colonia Centro

The most scenic location of this popular chain is on the eighth floor of a Sears, spilling onto a breezy terrace with an unobstructed view of Bellas Artes and Alameda Park. Named after the authoritarian president who industrialized Mexico, it's a charmer for a quick pick-me-up while eating

and sightseeing across the Centro—try one of their elaborate hot or cold chocolate drinks (with ingredients like achiote and flor de cacao, a plant unrelated to cacao), or a boozy coffee, with pastries or a glistening fruit tart.

6. El Gallo de Oro
Calle de Venustiano Carranza 35, colonia Centro

Most visit El Gallo de Oro (the Golden Chicken), in operation since 1874, for its history, though the cabrito (baby goat) has never left the menu and has many fans. Meat lovers can start here with morcilla (blood sausage) imported from Burgos, Spain, then move on to one of three parrilladas, or grilled meat platters. A daily four-course set lunch menu is a bargain.

7. Lady Tacos de Canasta
Francisco I. Madero 7, colonia Centro

Street food maven and LGBTQ activist Marven won viral fame in 2019 with her appearance on the Netflix series *Taco Chronicles*, but it's her tacos that keep fans coming back. Inside the bright purple and pink interior are traditional steamed tacos of everything from simple potato or bean to chicharrón prensado (a kind of pork terrine) and even iguana. Her salsa de chile cuaresmeño (aka jalapeño) is a hit with fans of this charismatic figure.

8. Limosneros
Ignacio Allende 3, colonia Centro

Designed by Juan Pablo Ballesteros in a four-century-old building, with an eye-catching look that blends contemporary fixtures into the historic stone walls, Limosneros proudly reimagines traditional Mexican dishes in a fine-dining context.
Try twenty-one-day-aged duck breast over a chile chilhuacle sauce sweetened with piloncillo (unrefined sugar), or delicate sliced hamachi dressed with flecks of chile chiltepín (a tiny, hot dried chile) in a white bean miso. Starters include Oaxacan-inspired croquettes filled with tasajo (cured beef), and many dishes feature Indigenous delicacies like acociles (crayfish), cocopaches (beetles), and escamoles (ant eggs). Pair all with some mezcal, Mexican wine, or inventive cocktails for an ideal date night.

9. Masala y Maíz
Calle Artículo 123 116, colonia Centro

One of the city's most acclaimed and forward-thinking restaurants, Masala y Maíz merges owners Norma Listman's and Saqib Keval's backgrounds for a unique convergence of South Asian, East African, and Mexican cuisines. It also maintains a focus on environmental, labor, and social justice, both within the restaurant industry and globally. Evocatively named dishes—matoke mixiote, pipián paneer, esquites (see page 42) makai pakka—only hint at the complexity on the plates. Opt for a tasting menu for the best experience.

10. Migas La Güera
Toltecas 12, colonia Morelos

In 1967, the late Celia Patiño "La Güera" López started selling migas, a slow-cooked pork bone soup thickened with migas (breadcrumbs) and seasoned with lots of epazote (a Mexican herb), in the tianguis of Barrio Tepito. It spurred a tradition that never quite escaped the confines of Tepito, making migas something of a neighborhood specialty. The tradition lives on with her son, José Luis Frausto Patiño, on Toltecas street, where the hearty soup sells out every day. Arrive early—Tepito locals like migas for breakfast—and order a bowl with a pork bone full of marrow, garnished to your taste. Late arrivals will miss the bones, but a bowl of migas solas, without bones, is just as good. Pickled pig trotter and pig skin tostadas are recommended appetizers, on crunchy tortillas layered with queso blanco and crema.

11. Migas Mary
Avenida del Trabajo
at Calle Caridad,
colonia Morelos

Founded in 1913, this acclaimed fonda for migas, the pork bone soup thickened with breadcrumbs that's so popular in Tepito, likewise serves an outstanding bowl of pancita (see page 151). There is only one decision to make, small or large, before a hot bowl of beef stomach soup with various offal cuts—beef tendon is popular for its texture—is served with lime wedges, blackened chile de árbol, Mexican oregano, chopped onions, and salsa roja to make a complex, spicy mix. Small portions of migas and pancita here might be the best one-two breakfast punch in town.

12. Paxia
Venustiano Carranza 69,
colonia Centro

Chef Daniel Ovadía leans back into Mexican flavors and traditions at this relaunch of his seminal

flagship restaurant whose original location closed in 2015. The precisely executed tasting menu features smart takes on classic dishes like an octopus gordita (see page 42), torta ahogada (see page 42), and mole chichilo (one of Oaxaca's classic mole sauces) with short rib, accompanied by Mexican wines. The restaurant has an amazing view of Centro, so try booking just before sunset.

13. El Pozole de Moctezuma
Moctezuma 12,
colonia Guerrero

Though it's been around since the 1940s, El Pozole de Moctezuma still feels like a secret: There are no signs, and to enter you have to ring the buzzer of a nondescript apartment building. Pozole fans, however, are well aware of what's probably the best version of this pork-and-hominy stew in the city. The Guerrero-style green pozole, thickened with pumpkin seeds, comes with lime, chile, oregano, onion, avocado, raw egg, chicharrón (pork rind; ask for it "carnudo," with some meat

still attached), and sardines in oil or tomato sauce.

14. Quesadillas Cuba
República de Cuba 99,
colonia Centro

At the corner of República de Cuba and República de Brasil, under a canopy of bright blue umbrellas, find quesadillas filled with quelites (wild greens), flor de calabaza (squash blossom), and huitlacoche (see page 56), among other antojitos (see page 53), plus pambazos (see page 42) and chilaquiles. The stand, founded thirty-two years ago by the late Maria Natalia Rocha, has been run by her daughter-in-law, Elizabeth Tovar, for the past sixteen years.

15. Ricos Tacos Toluca
López 103,
colonia Centro

This is Mexican street food charcuterie at its finest. Go all in at Ricos Tacos Toluca for rare chorizo verde, queso de puerco (head cheese), or obispo (white pork sausage) mixed with fries, piled in corn tortillas, and dressed with spicy guacamole and bright salsas made by Rosa González. Ted Oliver Rossano opened his original stand in 2003 and recently moved down the street into a larger space complete with an attractive new logo: a yin-and-yang featuring intertwined green and red chiles, the duality of spice.

16. Salón Familiar La Mascota

Mesones 20,
colonia Centro

The very loose rule at the 1920s-era cantina is that for every three drinks you get a free botana (see page 53), perhaps spicy snails, beef fritters in salsa verde, tuna-stuffed avocado, or tostadas de pata (cow's foot). After a few rounds, the snacks come faster than you can drink, though the camaraderie keeps you in the spirit to order more tequilas, micheladas, or Cuba libres.

17. Tacos de Canasta El Flaco

Calle 5 de Febrero 15-19,
colonia Centro

Just a stone's throw from the Zócalo is a convenient stop for tacos de canasta (see page 117), or basket tacos, packed with adobo, mole verde, papa, frijol, or chicharrón (pork rinds), the standard menu selection of these steamed tacos in Mexico's capital. For more than sixty years, the González family has run this petite stall where soft, steamed tacos are winnowed from an insulated box. Customers can fill or top their stacks of tacos with a very spicy salsa de aguacate (avocado), and pickled chiles and vegetables are available to snack on between bites.

18. Tacos El Puma

Luis González Obregón 5a,
colonia Centro

On the Luis González Obregón side of República de Brasil across from Plaza de Santo Domingo is a small taquería offering tacos a la plancha (see page 121), but upon closer inspection there are a bunch of clay casserole dishes bursting with vivid guisados (stews) like chicharrón (pork rinds) en salsa verde, tortas de pollo, and costillas en salsa roja, to be spooned onto corn tortillas with a bed of

Mexican rice to trap the delicious liquids in the taco. Look for up to nine guisados that change often at this tiny stall conveniently located a short walk from the Zócalo.

19. Taquería Coco-Loco

Mercado 14 de Tepito
Toltecas 24, locales 180–182,
colonia Morelos

Operating out of the Mercado de Tepito for more than thirty years, this spot propelled "quesocarnes" to their current popularity. Here, sloppy tacos are made with a juicy blend of ground

22. Tripolandia
Plaza Juan José Baz 5,
colonia Centro

Innards are always in fashion for chilangos (see page 54), and tripas (see page 57) connoisseurs have been coming to this tiny storefront in Plaza Juan José Baz since 1955. Generous tacos of tripas are cooked here just the way the customer likes: soft or crispy, in large pieces, or finely chopped. Top them with pápalo (an earthy wild herb) and a fiery salsa de chile de árbol, and plan on standing while eating, since the limited seating will likely be occupied.

beef and chopped onions, and smothered in piles of melty quesillo (Oaxacan string cheese). Rows of blistered flour tortillas flecked with burnt bits of meat and onions are packed with a lavish amount of filling and given a final toast on the plancha before being dressed with pickled cactus, pickled onion and habanero slices, and a spicy salsa verde. There's also a mushroom option for vegetarians.

20. Taquería El Torito
Mesones 48,
colonia Centro

Since 1957, this busy taquería on Isabel La Católica founded by Benigno Lares, now run by his grandchildren, has had a following due to its unusual tacos campechanos of suadero (see page 57) with tripas (see page 57), each cooked in separate comales (see page 55) in their respective fats to retain their distinct flavors. Regulars start with a plate

of four—anything less is a missed opportunity.

21. Tezontle
Rinconada de Jesús 7,
colonia Centro

One of the city's most underrated tasting menus is the ten-course chef's counter at Tezontle, a sunny restaurant atop the hotel Casa de la Luz. Chefs Ezequiel Garnica and Jorge Sibaja are both from Oaxaca, and their food combines Oaxacan tradition with the diversity of ingredients in CDMX: Look for dishes like grasshopper-crusted tuna aguachile (see page 53) with passion fruit and mango, and split pea sopes topped with fried octopus, chorizo, and habanero chile ash. It's also a terrific choice for breakfast before a day of sightseeing in Centro; try the Chilaquiles Tezontle (with pasilla chile sauce and salt-cured beef).

CENTRO HISTÓRICO
SHOPPING

The Centro Histórico is about tradition, and the best shopping here is as well. (Tip: Many of the area's fifty-plus museums have interesting shops, like Museo Franz Mayer and Museo de Arte Popular.) Allow yourself time to really roam these markets, talk to vendors, and look beyond the flashier stalls that tend to be near the entrances.

1. Mercado de Artesanías La Ciudadela
Balderas and Emilio Donde, colonia Centro
There's no better place for one-stop souvenir shopping than this massive crafts market across from a lovely park. While there aren't a lot of things that are impossible to find elsewhere, the variety here is unparalleled, it's all made in Mexico, and it's all fairly priced.

2. Mercado de la Merced
Circunvalación, La Merced Centro Histórico colonia Centro
The biggest public market in Mexico takes up so much of the southeast corner of the Centro Histórico that the

neighborhood itself is called La Merced. With more than four thousand vendors, it can be daunting for some, but it's a requisite pilgrimage for market devotees.

3. Mercado San Juan E. Pugibet
Segunda Calle de Ernesto Pugibet 21, colonia Centro

This market was once four separate markets, which were consolidated with this name under three buildings in the 1950s as the streets around them developed. One area is dedicated to more traditional food, one features crafts and antiques, one stocks flowers, and the other is the one you're looking for. You'll usually hear it called, simply, "Mercado San Juan," and it's often referred to as the "chef's market" for gourmet and imported ingredients—hard-to-find seafood like barnacles and live scallops, insects considered delicacies, game meats, and so on.

4. Mercado Sonora
Fray Servando Teresa de Mier 419, colonia Merced Balbuena

Located just south of Mercado de la Merced, this is known as the "witches' market" for its focus on herbal medicine and anything else you might need for healing ceremonies of all persuasions, including live animals. Go with an open mind.

5. Tianguis La Lagunilla
Comonfort 32, colonia Morelos

This sprawling Sunday flea market is the city's largest and most diverse in its offerings. Food-minded bargain hunters might find vintage tools and cookware, well-loved molcajetes and metates (stone grinders), piloncillo (sugar) molds, tin beer signs, century-old serving pieces, cookbooks, crystal stemware, and manual coffee mills.

BEYOND RESTAURANTS

Coffee Shops
Balam Coffee Roasters
Café Jekemir
Café Regina
Curva Café

Bars
Bósforo
La Bótica Centro
Museo del Tequila y el Mezcal
Pulquería Las Duelistas
Salón Bach
Terraza Gran Hotel
Zinco Jazz Club

Bakeries
Pastelería Ideal Centro
Pastelería Madrid
La Vasconia

Sweets
Dulcería La Celaya
Finca Rocío Chocolate
Kuxtal Chocolatería Artesanal

MEXICO CITY ESSENTIALS

STREET FOOD

In Mexico City, "street food" is both a literal reality (food prepared and served on the street) and a concept (hand-friendly food served in markets and casual restaurants). Mexican street food encompasses the standard antojitos (page 53) as well as hot dogs, hamburgers, and everything from street sushi (a thing) to the juice stands that are as ubiquitous in the city as taquerías. The following common street dishes, which you'll see throughout the city, are must-tries.

- **Elote:** Corn on the cob, usually with mayo, crumbled cheese, and other toppings.

- **Esquites:** Off the cob, served in a cup with similar toppings. For more, see page 55.

- **Gordita:** Masa dough stuffed with filling, patted into a round shape, and fried in oil. To garnish, the vendor slices partway around the perimeter and places salsas and other garnishes inside.

- **Huarache:** A huge oval tortilla, so named for its resemblance to the sole of a shoe ("huarache" means sandal), cooked on a comal with various toppings. Something like a large **sope** (see below).

- **Pambazo:** A torta-adjacent sandwich coated in salsa and seared on a comal. **Tortas ahogadas** are similar but saucier and, usually, spicier.

- **Quesadilla:** A tortilla folded around a filling and heated on a comal (page 55). In CDMX, quesadillas—despite the fact that queso (cheese) is in the name—don't automatically come with cheese. Raw tortilla dough that's been filled, sealed, and fried in oil is a **quesadilla frita**. Cheese sandwiched between two flour tortillas is usually called a **sincronizada**.

- **Sope:** A thick, flat tortilla with pinched edges, cooked on a comal with various toppings (also sometimes called **garnacha**, **picada**, **memela**, or **pellizcada**).

- **Taco:** A tortilla folded or rolled around a filling. A taco made with a flour tortilla and melted cheese is called a **gringa**. For more, see page 114.

- **Tamal:** Masa dough whipped with lard or other saturated fat (e.g., coconut oil, shortening) wrapped in corn husks, banana leaves, or other material. Usually the masa is folded over a simple meat or vegetable filling, and steamed. "Tamal" is singular; "tamales" is plural.

- **Tlacoyo:** Masa dough stuffed with a filling, patted into an oval shape, and cooked on a dry comal. Garnishes (which usually include nopales) are placed on top (shown opposite).
- **Torta:** A sandwich made on one of two crusty rolls, bolillos (torpedo-shaped and crunchier) or teleras (rounder and softer). Generally, these are filled with a protein and sometimes cheese, in addition to extra ingredients like beans, avocado, chiles, lettuce, and/or tomato. A torta filled with a tamal is called a **guajolota**.

The classic food trucks that represent Mexican street food for most people in the US are all but nonexistent in Mexico. Instead, the street stands (called puestos) usually have fixed locations—which some have held for decades—often with stools so you can sit semi-comfortably while you eat. These may be shacks with fairly extensive kitchens, or just an umbrella over a coal-fired comal. Most of the permanent covered indoor markets have sections with dozens of puestos, as well as others scattered around the market.

In general, you eat at the stand, availing yourself of the salsas, lime wedges, and other garnishes, then pay when you're done (because, after all, you may want another taco). You'll likely receive your order on a plastic bag-covered plastic plate or something akin to it, which you return when you're done. Despite many tourist guides' efforts to codify the Mexican street food experience, there aren't any rules beyond what you would do anywhere you order at a counter: Ask questions (or point), be polite, and avoid stands with no customers at peak hours.

At the weekly street markets called tianguises (see page 57) that are held in most neighborhoods, there are street stands that are put up just for that day. These are often, effectively, sprawling outdoor restaurants that may seat fifty or more people, some even with menus and table service.

A place that primarily serves tacos is, of course, a taquería. An antojería is the word for a place that serves a range of antojitos, but you rarely see or hear the word; you'd say "Let's go get huaraches" rather than "I feel like visiting an antojería." Along the same lines, "vitamina T"—the cute term for antojitos, since the core ones start with a *T*—is something you might see referenced on social media or blogs but isn't much used in everyday speech or on signage.

Finally, don't be apprehensive about eating on the street. Many people do so daily, meat is almost always cooked well done (or close to it), and the last thing a puesto owner wants is for word to get out that their food is unsanitary.

REGIONAL MEXICAN

Like most large countries' cuisines, Mexican cooking is a collection of regional cuisines that share some similarities but have distinct ingredients and dishes. CDMX is the only city in the country where foods from every region (and regions within regions) are well represented. When speaking about the city's culinary diversity, we are talking about the diversity of Mexican food as well. Here are some of the key regions to know.

Jalisco

Many Mexican cultural icons originated in Jalisco—mariachi, sombreros, charreada (Mexican rodeo)—and though the historian jury is out as to whether these foods were invented within Jalisco's present-day borders, it's the spiritual home of equally iconic dishes like birria, pozole, and tortas ahogadas (page 42). It's the country's leading state in terms of food production, a major source of cattle, pork, seafood, corn, rice, sugar cane, tomatoes, and chiles. **Birria la Jalisciense** (page 149) serves beef birria, best ordered tatemado (charred and crisped). **El Pialadero de Guadalajara** is a one-stop trip to Jalisco's capital city, with tortas ahogadas, carne en su jugo, birria, pozole, and barbacoa (see page 116)—a meat-centric menu, but shrimp and vegetarian tortas

ahogadas are available. **Pozolería Jalisco** (page 152) has Jalisco-style pozole and birria, but don't miss the jalisquilla, a sincronizada (see page 42) filled with birria.

Dishes to look for: birria (chile-braised meat), pozole (hominy stew), tortas ahogadas (salsa-drenched tortas), caldo michi (a fish soup), carne en su jugo (beef and beans)

El Pialadero de Guadalajara
Hamburgo 332, colonia Juárez

Norteño

The arid desert of much of inland northern Mexico isn't great for tropical produce or seafood. Instead, it's the land of cattle ranching, and wheat instead of corn. The beef is among the world's best, historically cooked outdoors (carne asada) or dried (machaca), and the tortillas are made of flour and beef fat, pork lard, or butter. **Los de Asada** (page 116) is modeled after norteño grills, and you can order both whole cuts and tacos. **Norteñito Steak** (page 131) has beefy tacos, burritos, and even empalmes, a lesser-seen snack from the state of Nuevo León consisting of beans, cheese, and sometimes meat sandwiched between two lard-fried corn tortillas. **Parrilla Raider** (page 65) is a weekend market puesto with real charcoal-grilled beef in cuts like aguja norteña and

Argentina-style chistorra (thin pork sausage).

Dishes to look for: carne asada (grilled beef), cabrito (baby goat), discada (a kind of large, meaty stir-fry), machaca con huevo (dried beef and eggs)

Oaxaca

Oaxacan is probably the most well-known regional cuisine in Mexico, though there's a lot of variety within the state due to its varied topography and many Indigenous communities. It's sometimes called "land of the seven moles" for the seven signature types, from green to jet black. The rich and complex cuisine is largely based around dried chiles, nuts, seeds, herbs, and spices that are less seen elsewhere in Mexico. At **Corazón de Maguey** (page 108), enjoy Oaxacan snacks meant to be eaten with their extensive mezcal menu, like guacamole with chapulines (grasshoppers), and molotes (plantain fritters with mole negro).

Guzina Oaxaca (page 85) showcases the best of upscale Oaxacan that never sidelines tradition. The hybrid Mexican-Oaxacan cuisine at **Mixtli** (page 131) is fresh and comforting rather than gimmicky.

Dishes to look for: manchamanteles (a fruity mole), sopa de guías (squash-vine soup), tlayudas (large comal-crisped tortillas with layers of toppings, shown at left), enmoladas (tortillas in mole sauce)

Sinaloa

The coastal Pacific state of Sinaloa may have usurped Oaxaca as the state with CDMX's current favorite regional cuisine. While there are meaty dishes like chilorio (pork in chile sauce), it's largely seafood, and most of the city's casual seafood restaurants are based on—or heavily reference—Sinaloan-style raw and gently cooked shrimp, scallop, skate, marlin, snapper, bass, and other marine dishes. **Mi Compa Chava** (page 15 and 109) is best for groups, to share all the wild combinations and portions, though it never compromises on the quality of the base ingredients. **Playas D' Sinaloa** prides itself on offering every raw or cooked seafood dish from the region, in generous portions and seasoning that exists only to enhance the seafood's freshness.

And at **El Sabalito** (page 153), enjoy aguachile tostadas with cooked dishes like snapper filets smothered in garlic and chile.

Dishes to look for: aguachile (see page 53), caguamanta (a seafood stew), tacos gobernadores (cheesy fish tacos), pescado zarandeado (fire-grilled whole fish)

Playas D' Sinaloa
Multiple locations,
playasdesinaloa.com.mx

Veracruz

A long, thin state along Mexico's eastern coast, this is where Spanish explorer Hernán Cortés first touched land in Mexico and established it as a major throughway for Spanish settlers and traders. Accordingly, the cuisine reflects strong influences from Spanish immigrants and enslaved West Africans—peanuts, sesame, tamarind, plantains, capers, olives, garlic, raisins—plus the many fish and shellfish off its coastline.

La Embajada Jarocha has live music and all the seafood soups and stews the state is known for. Order the plato jarocho (the latter meaning "from Veracruz"), an assortment of Veracruz-style antojitos (page 53), at **La Fonda del Recuerdo**.

Dishes to look for: pescado a la veracruzana (fish in an olive-caper sauce), chilpachole de jaiba (crab in a spicy tomato broth), huatape (a corn-thickened seafood stew), arroz a la tumbada (a brothy seafood rice).

La Embajada Jarocha
Zacatecas 138, colonia Roma Norte

La Fonda del Recuerdo
C. Río Lerma 170, colonia Cuauhtémoc

Yucatán

The Yucatán península—made up of three states that border Guatemala and Belize (Campeche, Yucatán, and Quintana Roo)—has a fresh, vibrant cuisine that seems a mix of those of its Mexican, Central American, and Caribbean neighbors, along with deep-rooted Lebanese influences from years of immigration. Here, fruity but deadly habaneros are the fresh pepper of choice, sour oranges dominate over limes, and earthy achiote seeds are often used where dried chiles would be elsewhere in Mexico. **Los Almendros** (page 107) was a pioneer in placing Yucatecan cuisine in a formal restaurant context, and it's still a perfect spot for a leisurely and/or power lunch. Something about the acid, salt, and fat in so many Yucatecan dishes makes them fit for drinking with, so a Yucatecan cantina like **Montejo** (page 15) always fits the bill; try the panuchos de cazón (fried bean-stuffed tortillas topped with shark). And if you want a textbook cochinita pibil, **El Turix** (page 87) is the place.

Dishes to look for: cochinita pibil (long-cooked pork), poc chuc (quick-cooked sour orange–marinated pork), pescado tikin-xic (achiote grilled fish), panuchos (fried bean-stuffed tortillas with garnishes)

Los Almendros
Avenida Insurgentes Sur 1759, colonia Guadalupe Inn

SPANISH

As progressive as the Mexico City restaurant scene is, the city's Spanish restaurants tend more toward tradition than the innovation that characterizes modern Spanish cuisine in Spain. Like French restaurants, Spanish restaurants long represented a certain luxury that was in opposition to the Mexican or Indigenous food that tended to be associated with the lower classes.

Spanish food is most visible in cantinas (page 139), which are emblematic of Mexico, but the older ones especially retain many Spanish dishes like tortilla española, salt cod fritters, porky caldo gallego, and Spanish chorizo (see page 55) braised in cider.

There is still a conversation between Spanish and Mexican cuisine in the city, though most locals will bemoan Spanish food's lack of heat and acid. On typically Mexican menus you might see such Spanish dishes as rice, both soupy (arroz caldoso) and dry (arroz seco; i.e., paella), garlic shrimp in clay cazuelas, croquettes, stewed and grilled octopus, Spanish cheeses, hams, and wines. Even Contramar (page 13), that bastion of Mexican seafood, has Spanish-style tuna croquettes and the Spanish taberna standard huevos rotos (eggs over French fries with jamón serrano).

Fitting its luxe Polanco setting, **La Barra de Fran** beautifully straddles tradition with innovation and top-quality ingredients. With three locations, **Bulla**, from Spanish chef Pedro Martín, is a satisfying spot for some tapas and wine or a full-on meal, with many ingredients imported directly from Spain, like the famed blood sausage of Burgos. Think of **Casiño Espanol de México** as much as a museum as a restaurant: Go for the art and furnishings; stay for the food. **Zeru** offers a survey of both Basque and pan-Spanish food, with specialties such as whole fish, Mexican and imported beef, and rice dishes like the mixed-seafood black rice with a punchy aioli.

La Barra de Fran
Avenida Emilio Castelar 185, colonia Polanco

Bulla
Multiple locations, bulla.mx

Zeru
Monte Everest 635, colonia Lomas de Chapultepec

JAPANESE

The Japanese influence on Mexico City's cuisine and culture is deeply rooted and well integrated. Ingredients like soy sauce, miso, seaweed, and sashimi-style fish are worked into Mexican dishes without a hint of novelty, and in return, Japanese restaurants highlight Mexican fruits, chiles, and herbs. It's a fascinating, unexpected aspect of the city to keep an eye out for. Read more about Mexico City's affinity for Japanese cooking (and restaurants) on page 99.

SEAFOOD

Mexico City's fish market is the second largest in the world by volume, and despite being landlocked, Mexico City is one of the world's best cities for seafood of all types, both imported and from Mexico's endless coastlines. Read more about the seafood market that's made CDMX a marine mecca, and where to eat there, on page 157.

SWEETS

Any busy city block will have some combination of bakeries, coffee shops, corner stores, and street vendors offering sugary treats at any time of day. In the morning, among those selling tamales and tacos de canasta (see page 117) are vendors with huge baskets of pan dulce, sweet breads and pastries that might include conchas (fluffy round buns with a thin sugar coating), cuernos (akin to croissants), orejas (akin to palmiers), garibaldis (kind of like cupcakes covered in tiny sugar pearls), or just crusty rolls slathered in jam.

Stop first at **Pastelería Suiza** (not a Swiss bakery per its name, but when it opened in 1942, the owner thought that "Swiss" represented quality) for a look at the entire range of sweet (and some savory) Mexican baked goods: pastries, cookies, pies, tarts, chocolate, candied fruit, and much more. But most of the best pastries are at bakeries helmed by a younger generation bringing obsessive technique to classic Mexican baking, with Paris-worthy laminated doughs and long-fermented sourdoughs, like at **Da Silva**, **Ficelle**, and **Saint**.

Pastelería Suiza
Parque España 7, colonia Condesa

Da Silva
Oscar Wilde 8, colonia Polanco

Ficelle
Avenida Tamaulipas 39b, colonia Condesa

Saint
Benjamín Hill 146, colonia Condesa

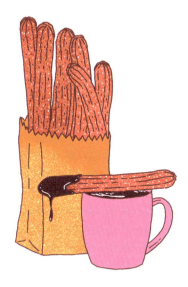

Ice creams are generally sold as nieves (water-based) and helados (milk-based), though it's reductive to call them sorbets and ice creams, since nieves are usually less icy and more fruit-intensive than most sorbets, and helados often have a higher concentration of the base ingredient (fruits or nuts, for example), as opposed to stretching the flavor out with cream. Paletas are ice pops and are expected to be made with fresh ingredients. **Nevería Roxy** started in 1946, but by the old-school look of some of their locations, you'd think it was a century earlier. Always made with fresh ingredients puréed in small ten-liter batches, the treats at Roxy still represent for many locals the pinnacle of fruit purity in frozen confections.

Nevería Roxy
Eight locations, neveriaroxy.com.mx

Churros are a Spanish import, and though you'll find vendors in markets and subway stations with passable versions, **Churrería El Moro** is the obligatory stop for churro and chocolate fans. Here they're piped out daily into huge spirals that are cut into serving sticks to dunk into one of five rich-n-thick, hot or cold chocolate styles. All fifteen locations are top-quality, but the original has the best atmosphere.

Churrería El Moro
Eje Central Lázaro Cárdenas 42, colonia Centro

DRINKING

Whether you partake or not, drinking culture is an important window into Mexico City and its people. The maguey (agave)—the base of mezcal, tequila, and pulque —is as symbolic of Mexico as corn and chile; before the Spanish conquests (see page 22), it was a source of food and drink, needle and thread, weapon and armor. Wine was made in Mexico long before the United States, and the oldest still-operating winery in the Americas is in Mexico. The city's mixology scene is gaining international attention with its use of traditional ingredients and techniques. And of course, Mexican beers are among the world's most consumed. Cantinas (see page 138) are the heart of Mexico City drinking culture, but that's just the beginning.

Mezcal

Though only certain states are allowed to put "mezcal" on the label, mezcal is any distillate made from cooked agave hearts (tequila is one type of mezcal made from one specific agave, only in authorized states). For all the ubiquity of mezcal in contemporary spirit circles, it's only been about twenty years that mezcal has been appreciated as an artisanal product among most Mexicans. Prior to that, it was viewed as a sort of Oaxacan moonshine due to the poor versions that dominated the market. Now, the country's priciest resorts tout their mezcal selections, and the finest restaurants offer it to open and close tasting menus. It's a popular ingredient in cocktails, but quality mezcal is best enjoyed straight (no ice), and is typically served with orange slices and salt, which may be flavored with such ingredients as insects, chiles, or burnt tortillas. **Ticuchi** (page 87) has a terrific selection among a menu of mostly vegetarian, mostly snacky dishes. **La Clandestina** and **El Palenquito**, from the same team, offer unbranded mezcals sourced directly from the producers, with detailed information about each, and an exceptionally informed staff.

La Clandestina
Avenida Álvaro Obregón 298, colonia Condesa

El Palenquito
Avenida Álvaro Obregón 39, colonia Roma Norte

Pulque

Another intoxicating agave product is pulque, the fermented sap of certain large agaves and both a healthful and entertaining beverage in pre- and post-Hispanic Mexico. It's a 100 percent natural product, which starts as a sweet liquid and ferments naturally, gaining strength with each day (it's usually served at a strength akin to a weak beer). In the late 1800s there were multiple pulquerías on every block, while now there are only a handful, though restaurant and bar owners who promote Indigenous products are working hard to ensure that real pulque—it resists canning and other methods of preservation—doesn't disappear. Founded in 1912, **Pulquería Las Duelistas** is one of the few remaining historic pulquerías and still draws a lively daytime crowd, ranging from teenagers in tribal tattoos to elderly men taking a quiet break. When **Pulquería Los Insurgentes** opened in 2010, many people balked at the idea of reviving pulque as a "cool" drink, but it's still going strong.

Pulquería Las Duelistas
Aranda 28, colonia Centro

Pulquería Los Insurgentes
Avenida Insurgentes Sur 226, colonia Roma Norte

Wine

Though Mexico still isn't a huge consumer of wine, there's been an explosion of wine bars in the past several years (whether serving natural, Mexican, or international wines), and wine has become more of a focus on higher-end restaurant drink menus. Wine has deep history in Mexico—it was introduced with the Spanish, and the still-extant Casa Madero, in Coahuila state, dates to 1597—and there's been increased appreciation for it both as a historic product and as one with limitless potential in the global wine world. More than 75 percent of Mexican wine is from Valle de Guadalupe (near Ensenada, in northern Baja California), and states like Querétaro, Coahuila, and San Luis Potosí are emerging with wines grown at altitudes that mitigate temperatures that would otherwise be too hot for great wine. Look for it on restaurant menus, or pick up some bottles to taste at the all-Mexican **La Contra**, or **Vinos Chidos**, a shop specializing in small, naturally minded producers.

La Contra
Jalapa 129, colonia Roma Norte

Avenida Miguel Hidalgo 9, colonia Del Carmen

Vinos Chidos
Multiple locations, vinoschidos.mx

Cocktails

When the cocktail bar **Limantour** opened in colonia Roma in 2011, it marked Mexico City's entrée into global mixology circles, making impeccable classic cocktails and new inventions like a margarita with flavors pulled from tacos al pastor (see page 120). Since then, the city's cocktail and culinary cultures have developed along parallel lines, finding more success looking inward than out. To use one measure, on North America's 50 Best Bars list, Mexico City has more than any other North American city except New York.

Baltra, on a shady Condesa side street, uses Mexican flavors like guanábana (soursop), achiote (annatto seed), jasmine, and tepache (see page 57) in drinks that straddle classic and tiki. The drinks at **Las Brujas** are sometimes named for the Latin American women who inspired them, like the Ángela Vicario (a Gabriel García Marquéz protagonist), a mix of citrus blossoms and lemongrass with tequila. At **Handshake Speakeasy**, try agave spirits with powerful flavors like tomato, absinthe, and palo santo. **Hanky Panky** eschews cocktail snobbery in favor of a private-party vibe, and drinks that often incorporate herbs and spices like cardamom, thyme, cumin, coriander, curry, and lavender. And hit up **Rayo** in the early evening before the crowds descend, to focus on deeply Mexican drinks like sotol (a mezcal-adjacent spirit from Chihuahua state) with corn liquor and bitters made from the vaguely anisey herb hoja santa.

Limantour
Avenida Álvaro Obregón 106, colonia Roma Norte

Baltra
Iztaccihuatl 36D, colonia Condesa

Las Brujas
Río de Janeiro 56, colonia Roma Norte

Handshake Speakeasy
Amberes 65, colonia Juárez

Hanky Panky
Turín 52, colonia Juárez

Rayo
Salamanca 85, colonia Roma Norte

MEXICO CITY FOOD GLOSSARY

Aguachile: Aguachile is essentially just a spicy, chile-forward ceviche (citrus-marinated raw seafood). Yet perhaps because of the ongoing popularity of seafood from Sonora and Sinaloa states (where this dish originates), aguachile seems more common on the city's menus than raw fish dishes that are just labeled ceviche. Since some ceviches are spicy and some aguachiles are relatively mild, ceviches and aguachiles can be virtually interchangeable at some places. "Aguachile verde" or "rojo" refers to whether the heat comes from green or red chile.

Antojito: Think of antojitos, usually translated as "little cravings," as everything made with corn masa— tacos, tamales, tlacoyos, quesadillas, gorditas, garnachas, sopes, panuchos (fried, bean-stuffed tortillas), etc.— though the term also encompasses dishes made from flour tortillas (such as sincronizadas and gringas) and sandwiches like tortas and pambazos. These can be a tide-you-over snack between meals or, of course, meals in themselves. For explanations of some of the most popular antojitos, see the Street Food section on page 42.

Botana: An umbrella term for any small snack, this can encompass anything from peanuts at a bar to cocktail-party bites to elaborate small appetizers and amuse-bouches at upscale restaurants (antojitos, previous, are essentially a subset of botanas). At a cantina, traditionally, you're given a free botana with each drink, increasing in size and quality with each round, but like most traditions, this is no longer a given.

Café de olla: Traditionally brewed in a clay pot over direct heat, this mix of coffee with piloncillo (unrefined sugar) and canela (Mexican cinnamon) is a breakfast staple. Many restaurants in Mexico City serve café de olla and espresso, but not drip coffee.

Campechano: Somehow this word, which literally means "of or from the state of Campeche," came to mean, in culinary terms, a mixture. Usually, it refers to half and half: a Cuba campechana is rum with half Coke and half soda water, a cerveza campechana is light and dark beer. A taco campechano is usually chorizo or longaniza (see page 55) with a cut of beef (bistec, cecina, lengua), often with chicharrón (pork rinds) to make it a trio. A ceviche campechano, unless the kind of seafood is specified, usually includes a little of everything.

Champiñón/hongo/seta: All words for mushrooms, used more or less interchangeably. "Hongo" means fungus, so can be used more broadly, "champiñón" usually refers to common cultivated mushrooms, and "seta" is often used for wild mushrooms, but there are no firm rules here in everyday practice. Wild mushroom season is July to September.

Chapulines: Think of these grasshoppers (not crickets) as Oaxacan bacon bits. The insects are purged and cleaned, then fried with garlic, lime, and salt until dry and crisp, and used both as a primary protein source (in tacos, for example), or, more commonly in Mexico City, as a garnish for guacamole or an accompaniment to drinks, a la peanuts. Also see: Chicatanas, a large flying ant considered a seasonal delicacy, sold fried to be ground into salsas and moles.

Chela/cheve/caguama: Yes, beer is "cerveza," but you're more likely to hear one of these words for it. "Chela" is most common (cheve is somewhat associated

with the north of the country, and the related cheva with Yucatán), and caguama refers to the quart bottles that are used in markets to make micheladas. Cubeta isn't a word for beer, but for the bucket that you can buy, in some places, filled with beer bottles.

Chilango: Both the noun and the adjective ("chilango/a/x") for being from Mexico City, "chilango" was once a derogatory term used by people outside the city but has been reclaimed by locals. (A mainstream monthly arts and culture magazine called *Chilango* launched in 2003.) Other demonyms haven't caught on: "capitalino" is considered formal and potentially confusing for other state and country capitals; "defeño" makes less sense since the city's name was legally changed in 2016 from Distrito Federal (D.F.) to Ciudad de Mexico (CDMX); the recently proposed "mexiqueño" presents obvious problems for foreigners. The city is sometimes slangily called "Chilangolandia." Not all residents of the metropolitan area—which includes fifty-nine municipalities in the State of México and one in Hidalgo state—agree on whether they should be considered chilangos or not.

Chile: Given the ubiquity and variety of chiles in Mexico, the actual word "chile" has little practical meaning. Rather than referring to chiles in terms of fresh versus dried, green versus red, or hot versus mild, you're far more likely to hear the specific chiles referenced, such as serrano, jalapeño, and poblano for fresh chiles, and ancho, guajillo, and pasilla for dried.

Chile cuaresmeño: The local word for jalapeño, since, after all, we're not in Jalapa, the city in Veracruz state where jalapeños hail from.

Chile morita/mora/meco/chipotle: Speaking of chiles, while "chipotle" is used in the United States for any dried, smoked chile, here they have different names depending on the base chile. Morita and mora (the former being smaller) are similar and considered the tastiest, while "meco" and "chipotle" are often used interchangeably, though "meco" can also sometimes refer to an unsmoked chile. Mexican chile nomenclature is always a moving target.

Chorizo/longaniza: These two words for fresh pork sausage seasoned with chiles and spices are almost synonymous: Longaniza, per its name, is simply tied in longer links than the ball-like chorizo. However, longaniza is usually a little fattier, and chorizo usually a little more powerfully spiced.

Comal: Call it a griddle if you must, but this is the disc (flat or with gently curving sides), usually made of clay or steel, used to make tortillas and other masa-based creations, and to dry-roast vegetables (see Tatemado, page 57).

Elote/esquites: Corn on the cob (elote) and off the cob (esquites) are both usually served with some mixture of lime, mayonnaise, queso fresco, and powdered chile to taste. People enamored of "Mexican street corn" are sometimes surprised to not see more elote and esquite vendors, but they usually emerge at night. Note that Mexican corn isn't bred for sugary sweetness, as in the United States, but instead has large, chewy kernels and a deeply savory flavor. Look for "Doriesquites," Doritos topped with esquites, with the frequent addition of peanuts and diced cucumber or jicama.

Escamoles: At first glance, this "Mexican caviar" looks like tiny corn kernels; in fact, it's ant larvae. Specifically, it's the larvae of certain ants that would be queen (only the queens' larvae are large enough to warrant harvesting; the mere commoners' larvae are just specks).

Mild and subtly sweet, they're generally served sautéed in butter and with the herb epazote, with tortillas to make tacos. Their high price is justified, since they must be harvested by hand during a short season (though they freeze well), leaving enough eggs to ensure a crop for the next year. They're a staple of high-end restaurants and a must-try.

Fonda: The small, inexpensive, lunch-only restaurants called fondas are slowly disappearing in upscale and touristy neighborhoods but are still a crucial part of daily life. Most serve comida corrida, a set menu of three to four courses, plus a pitcher of agua fresca.

Huitlacoche: Calling this corn fungus "Mexican truffle" does justice to neither; where truffles are incredibly aromatic but with little flavor, huitlacoche has little aroma but a rich earthy flavor, like a combination of fresh corn with wild mushroom. It can spontaneously arise on corn plants, but these days is more often inoculated to ensure its presence. It's usually a filling for quesadillas, but is sometimes puréed into sauces.

Prehispanic: This refers to anything before 1519, when Hernán Cortés arrived to conquer Mexico and rechristen it New Spain. From a culinary standpoint, it generally refers to Indigenous ingredients, techniques, and dishes.

Puesto: When you talk about street food in Mexico City, you're talking about puestos, stationary stands on the street or in markets, usually serving antojitos.

Quesadilla: Quesadillas in Mexico City don't always automatically include cheese, making them a perfect street snack for vegan friends (common veg fillings include squash blossom, huitlacoche, and mushroom). These folded and filled tortillas are usually griddled on a comal but occasionally deep-fried, like at the popular spot Quesadillas María Isabel. You'll sometimes hear the term slanged to "quekas" or "kekas."

Sobremesa: This is the post-dessert hang at a restaurant, usually over drinks, and a marathon sobremesa can even lead into another round of food. This is an expected part of a meal, which is why waiters here will virtually never bring the check without you requesting it.

Suadero: As one of the city's favorite taco fillings, suadero is a thing you'll hear mentioned often. Most butchers will tell you that it refers to one of two beef cuts: what is called rose meat in the United States and matambre elsewhere, a thin cut between the skin and ribs; or the front part of the belly that's sometimes labeled "plate" or "navel" in the States. In practice, however, taqueros use many different cuts that benefit from long, slow cooking, such as brisket, flank, and breast. It's generally cooked in a shallow moat of fat until tender, then chopped and crisped on the comal.

Taquear: Mexicans love to make verbs out of nouns, and "taquear"—to make tacos—is the most Mexican verb of all. "Taquería" (taco restaurant) and "taquero" (taco maker), of course, share the same root.

Tatemado: In Mexican cooking, tatemado falls somewhere between charred and burnt, a blackening technique (over fire, charcoal, or on a comal), which gives great depth to sauces and other dishes. Anything can be tatemado, but most common are vegetables like tomatoes, tomatillos, onions, garlic, and chiles, which are ground—blackened parts and all—into salsas.

Tepache: Tepache is an amber-colored drink made from fermented pineapple and piloncillo (unrefined cane sugar), usually with such a low alcohol content that it doesn't qualify as alcohol (kind of like a less tart kombucha). It's a common sight in street markets and is increasingly used as a cocktail ingredient.

Tianguis: From the Náhuatl word "tianquiztli" comes this term for the open-air or temporary markets that date to prehispanic times. Today, many neighborhoods have weekly pop-up markets they call tianguis, as opposed to mercados, which generally refer to the stationary covered neighborhood markets that are open daily.

Tripas: Despite the name, this very popular taco filling isn't tripe (that's pancita), but part of the small intestine, akin to chitterlings. They're usually beef, but sometimes pork.

Cuauhtémoc
Juárez
Renacimiento
San Rafael
Santa María La Ribera
Tabacalera
Zona Rosa

NEAR

3
NORTH

SANTA MARÍA
LA RIBERA

AV. RIBERA DE SAN COSME

SAN RAFAEL

CTO. INTERIOR MELCHOR OCAMPO

C. MAESTRO ANTONIO CASO

C. JAMES SULLIVAN

CUAUHTÉMOC

RENACIMIENTO

AV. INSURGENTES SUR

ZONA ROSA

AV. CHAPULTEPEC

NEAR NORTH

SHOPPING

1. Mercado de San Cosme
2. Museo del Chocolate
3. Plaza del Ángel
4. Quentín Miscelánea
5. Taller Lu'um
6. Utilitario Mexicano

DINING

1. Antojitos Yucatecos Los Arcos
2. Boca del Río
3. El Califa de León
4. Cantina La Castellana
5. Casa Bell
6. Cicatriz Café
7. Esquites Rul's
8. El Golfo de León
9. Hana Mart
10. Hiyoko
11. LENEZ
12. Mesón Puerto Chico
13. Parrilla Raider
14. Salón París
15. Le Tachinomi Desu
16. Tacos Don Memo
17. Taquería González
18. Taller de Ostiones by FISM
19. La Tonina
20. Wanwan Sakaba
21. Yi Pin Ju

TABACALERA

PASEO DE LA REFORMA

JUÁREZ

NEAR NORTH
DINING

There's a lot of action in this part of the city that lies north of Roma Norte, east of Chapultepec Park, and west of Centro. The many colonias here have distinct personalities, and often their character transforms from block to block.

Zona Rosa, the colloquial name for the western part of colonia Juárez, was once the heart of the area's LGBTQ community. Today, the faded sex shops, underwear stores, and internet cafés are joined by a mix of fast food, chain stores, a terrific antiques mall (Plaza del Ángel, especially good on Saturdays), and the city's Koreatown. Farther east, colonia Juárez feels a bit like an extension of Roma Norte, with stunning architecture, hip restaurants and cocktail bars, and the 2023 arrival of Soho House Mexico City, which marked the area's arrival as a tourist destination. At its northern edge, a row of corporate hotels along Paseo de la Reforma separates it from colonia Tabacalera, a business district centered around the phallic Monumento a la Revolución.

Colonia Cuauhtémoc is an upscale but mellow area of embassies and a cluster of the city's best Japanese restaurants that's been dubbed "Little Japan." Moving north, San Rafael is a colonia in transition, full of historic mansions, cantinas, churches, and theaters, alongside continuous new construction. Colonia Santa María la Ribera has been "about to happen" since the nineties, and its failure to gentrify like so many of its neighbors is one of its best qualities. In its center is a lovely park with an impressive Moorish kiosk, with various low-key restaurants and bars radiating off into its residential streets that house more than a few surprises.

3. El Califa de León
Avenida Ribera de San Cosme 56, colonia San Rafael

Supposedly the popular taco cut "gaonera"—thin-cut filet mignon—was invented here, named for the titular "Caliph of León," bullfighter Rodolfo Gaona. This little taquería has spawned several copycats, most notably the El Califa chain and El Faraón, which is sometimes called "El Califake," but this is the original and, arguably, the best (a reputation reinforced by its becoming the first taquería to receive a Michelin star, in 2024). Tortillas are made to order, and the stone-ground raw green salsa should be slathered on everything.

4. Cantina La Castellana
Maestro Antonio Caso 58, colonia San Rafael

One of the city's oldest cantinas (and a favorite among Revolution-era literary figures), La Castellana opened in 1892 but still has the exuberant feel of a new hotspot. Daily live music adds to the atmosphere, as does the great botana (see page 53) concept from two P.M. to six P.M. daily: Hit a (fairly reasonable) drink minimum per person, and the multicourse lunch menu that changes daily is on the house.

1. Antojitos Yucatecos Los Arcos
Florencia 43, colonia Juárez

As a rule, Yucatecan cuisine, with its finger-staining recados (seasoning pastes), stewed meats, and promiscuously garnished antojitos (see page 53, opts for flavor over being photogenic. So, it's only appropriate that some of the city's best is in this narrow storefront that promises little but delivers plenty. Come hungry, knowing that you'll order the chamorro pibil (slow-cooked pork shank), but start with any of the appetizers, like papadzules (egg tacos in creamy pumpkin-seed sauce) or pan de cazón (shark casserole).

2. Boca del Río
Avenida Ribera de San Cosme 42, colonia San Rafael

With so many hot new seafood restaurants in the city, it's easy to forget that fresh fish has been coming to restaurants here for several decades (see page 157). Boca del Río opened in 1941 and helped establish seafood cocktails, ceviches, and shrimp soup as Mexico City staples. With a lively, almost cantina-like atmosphere in the late afternoon, it's a fun place to drink beers and try dishes like whole fried fish, grilled langoustines, spiced broiled oysters "a la diabla," and chilpachole de jaiba, a crab soup from Veracruz.

coffee-and-pastry shop into a lunch and dinner destination that straddles New York and Mexico Cities—think chicken pot pie studded with chorizo (see page 55), roast carrots with tahini yogurt and salsa macha—then into one of the area's best cocktail and natural wine bars. It's a ritual among regulars to order the fried chicken sandwich to soak up the booze at the end of the night.

7. Esquites Rul's
Versalles 92, colonia Juárez
With three locations, chef Israel Ortiz's mini-chain of esquites (dressed corn kernels; see page 42) restaurants is a concept that's become a big hit in CDMX, elevating this popular street food tradition. There are plenty of elote and esquites vendors all over the city, but at Esquites Rul's you can make a meal out of esquites dressed with salsa macha

5. Casa Bell
Praga 14, colonia Juárez
It's getting harder to find old-school luxury restaurants, so it's nice to see that Casa Bell's popularity as a power-lunch spot continues unabated. The open-air courtyard is ringed by ornate birdcages filled with chirping birds whose discordant symphony makes a much better musical accompaniment than any piped-in playlist. The pato bell (minced duck

tacos) are a must to start, then move on to beef tenderloin in chipotle, sea bass a la veracruzana, or grilled octopus. With impeccable service, it's one of the city's best lunch picks on a beautiful day.

6. Cicatriz Café
Dinamarca 44, colonia Juárez
This bustling all-day café from chef-owner (and onetime Eater op-ed contributor) Scarlett Lindeman morphs from a morning

and mounted with bone marrow (shown opposite), suadero (see page 57), chicken gizzards, or chicken feet, plus sides of roasted baby corn dressed in chile mayo, and consomé de suadero (beef).

8. El Golfo de León
Joaquín Velázquez de León 79, colonia San Rafael

This bare-bones cantina seems to have changed little since opening in the 1930s and is all the better for it. Service is efficient and cheerful, drinks are fairly priced, botanas (see page 53) are extremely generous, and the à la carte menu of cantina classics like albondigas (meatballs) al chipotle, cabrito al horno (roast baby goat), and pulpo a la gallega (Galicia-style octopus) reads like Grandma's home cooking, with no cheffy riffs in sight.

9. Hana Mart
Londres 190-Local A, colonia Juárez

This is one of more than a dozen Korean grocers in the heart of colonia Juárez's Koreatown. Like most, it has a wide assortment of imported ingredients, snacks, and drinks, but what puts it above its competition is the generous take-out menu offered on weekends. Try delicately seasoned kimbap, just-grilled kalbi, or sticky pork legs. Pro tip on weekdays:

Buy a soju here and pour it into a thermos to bring to Antojitos Yucatecos Los Arcos (page 63) around the corner. Soju and chamorro pibil are a perfect pairing.

10. Hiyoko
Río Pánuco 132, colonia Cuauhtémoc

Order the chicken omakase at the bar here for a perfect illustration of the city's terrific Japanese food scene. It feels reductive to call Hiyoko simply a traditional yakitori restaurant; it's more of an intimate exploration of Jidori chicken. Try skewers of thigh and wing to start (grilled over binchō-tan charcoal, of course), then let the expert chefs prepare delicacies like heart, gizzard, neck skin, or cartilage. For variety, there are other creatures like duck and lamb, and enough vegetable skewers to satisfy vegetarian friends.

11. LENEZ
Londrez 207, colonia Juárez

Owner Wilton Romero Nava brings years of experience as a sommelier and wine distributor to LENEZ (a play on "the nose" in French), which has become a popular hangout for wine-industry professionals. It's ostensibly a wine bar, but the food is not to be missed, including an heirloom tomato carpaccio, mushroom croquettes, and a fried chicken sandwich with spicy salsa macha, which

pairs beautifully with an off-dry Riesling. The cellar holds more than six hundred labels—far more than most restaurants in the city.

12. Mesón Puerto Chico
José María Iglesias 55, colonia Tabacalera

Though it's less than thirty years old, Mesón Puerto Chico exudes nostalgia with its faithful take on an old-school Spanish inn, with arched doorways, leafy courtyards, and suited men bantering animatedly over several drinks. The menu leans to Northern Spain—morcilla de Villarcayo (a regional blood sausage), pulpo a la gallega (octopus with smoked paprika), Burgos-style suckling goat—but the appeal here is the atmosphere. It's part power lunch and part family celebration, and a reminder that the city's upscale restaurant scene didn't start ten years ago.

13. Parrilla Raider
James Sullivan 71, colonia San Rafael

On Saturdays and Sundays, next to the austere monolith to motherhood called Monumento a la Madre, the area around Jardín del Arte Sullivan park becomes a humming mostly food market. The tacos al carbón at this street stand are some of the city's best, a meat lover's dream with cuts that are rarely seen in the United

States, like aguja norteña, picaña, and Argentine-style chorizo (see page 55), and flour tortillas made to order. Wash it down with creative aguas frescas like mamey with coconut. For a break from red meat, the same owners have an excellent seafood stand in the market as well.

14. Salón París
Jaime Torres Bodet 151, colonia Santa María la Ribera

Though this legendary cantina moved into a new space across the street several years ago, it retains all its old-school charm and popular dishes like caldo de camarón (shrimp broth) and the fall-apart chamorro (pork shank). It's said to be the place where famed midcentury actor-singer José Alfredo Jiménez first performed, which is perhaps why there's always rousing ranchero and mariachi music, either via jukebox or roaming live musicians.

15. Le Tachinomi Desu
Río Pánuco 132-1a, colonia Cuauhtémoc

The folks behind the city's influential Edo Kobayashi restaurant group started this Japanese natural-wine-and-snacks bar in 2016 as a speakeasy, mostly for employees and friends to hang out after work. It's evolved into a destination bar, with the barely there "kitchen" behind the bar churning out dishes like okonomiyaki and truffled Wagyu sliders, and Japanese whiskies and tiny-production sakes in addition to the wine. It still retains the same intimacy, though, as if a friend snuck you into their restaurant to party after hours.

16. Tacos Don Memo
Calzada Manuel Villalongín 66, colonia Renacimiento

They say the first tacos sold in the city were tacos de canasta (see page 117). They keep for hours steaming under cloth in the basket, plus they're afford-able and portable, and it was easy for the seller to zip away on their bike if the authorities came to crack down on mobile vendors, as was once common. Don Memo's are textbook tacos de canasta—with a classic quintet of potato, bean, chicharrón (pork skin), mole verde, and adobo fillings—but the best reason to visit is that the tacos are so

damn delicious. Add your pick of three salsas: cooked green and red chile, and a pourable guacamole.

17. Taquería González
Bucareli and Donato Guerra, colonia Juárez

Veteran taquero Don Alberto González is a beloved figure for "los especiales," in which 250 grams of juicy hand-cut beef is seared on a comal and plated with a fistful of tortillas for making your own tacos. González butch-ers large slabs of steak to order, a cut he refers to as "rosbif" that he passes to his mulleted sidekick while asking diners if they want it medio (medium) or tres cuartos (medium well). Campechanos of rosbif with grilled longaniza for a little spice is another favorite taco among customers.

18. Taller de Ostiones by FISM
Versalles 113,
colonia Juárez

The best oysters in town are here, sent overnight from a farm in Baja California. Start with a large platter on the half shell, followed by the indulgent fried-oyster sandwich and maybe the "ostiones boneless," which are vastly better than the buffalo chicken nuggets they're modeled after. Also recommended is the owners' Barra California Sur by FISM in Santa María la Ribera, which is the same oyster-bar concept with more of a backyard-BBQ vibe. Both places are walk-in only, so build in a little wait time or a backup plan.

19. La Tonina
Serapio Rendon 27,
colonia San Rafael

The popular CDMX-born singer Thalía proclaimed this modest taquería her favorite childhood restaurant, and fans of northern-style tacos are likely to agree. Freshly made flour tortillas are stuffed with little-seen (in Mexico City) taco fillings like cabrito (goat), chilorio (chile-stewed pork), machaca con huevo (dried beef and eggs), frijoles maneados (creamy beans), and cochipecho, a Sonora-style mix of beef and pork in a red chile sauce. Construction workers start coming at nine A.M., followed by the late-morning hangover crowd, but it's best with a group so you can order one of everything.

20. Wanwan Sakaba
Londres 209,
colonia Juárez

A must if you're craving Japanese food (reinforced by the mostly Japanese clientele), Wanwan Sakaba has an exhaustive menu of sushi, sashimi, rice, and noodle dishes of all types, and more than thirty cooked meat and fish entrées. There's even a range of Chinese-style stir-fries, and motsuni, which they call "Japanese menudo," a tripe stew made with red miso. Still, befitting its name (which roughly translates to "bow wow bar"), it has the casual and occasionally rowdy spirit of a tavern, with long lists of sake, shochu, and Japanese whisky.

21. Yi Pin Ju
Londres 114,
colonia Juárez

There are too many great Chinese restaurants in Mexico City, representing many distinct Chinese cuisines, to proclaim any one of them as the best in the city. Still, Yi Pin Ju is a strong contender. Its Szechuan roots appeal to locals' affinity for heat: There's a brisk, fresh spiciness in the cucumber salad, chicken gizzards in an oily chile sauce that recalls salsa macha, and the anesthetizing sting of Szechuan peppercorns tossed with hand-stretched noodles.

67

NEAR NORTH
SHOPPING

Shopping in these busy neighborhoods is mostly centered around the modern malls Reforma 222 and Forum Buenavista, plus a seemingly endless array of Mexican and international chains. Still, there are always young residents and businesses arriving, which is why you'll see an elderly tailor next to a cutting-edge clothing designer.

1. Mercado de San Cosme
Gabino Barreda 18,
colonia San Rafael

Despite suffering considerable damage from a tragic fire in 2019, this market has reclaimed its position as one of the best in the city for eating, thanks to its several dozen puestos (see page 43). Still, the shopping is better than ever, with a focus on local farmers and a wide selection of organic and hard-to-find produce.

2. Museo del Chocolate
Calle Milan 45,
colonia Juárez

Don't miss this seductive museum devoted to chocolate, in a restored 1909 mansion. The nine rooms detail its history and production, plus there's an enclosed room with chocolate walls. Of course, this is a gift shop you don't want to miss, and there's also a drink window with several hot and cold cacao beverages on offer.

3. Plaza del Ángel
Londres 161,
colonia Juárez

Essentially a mall of long-standing antiques dealers, Plaza del Ángel is paradise for the upscale flea-market set (especially on Saturdays, when vendors spill out onto the common areas). This is the place to find antique crystal and cocktail sets, silver platters, and bateas (hand-painted wood trays from Michoacán).

4. Quentín Miscelánea
Bruselas 11,
Juárez

This terrific café and provisions store from a popular mini-chain of coffee shops (there are three other locations in Roma and Condesa) is ideal for edible souvenirs: salsas, honeys, jams, spices, tinned fish, olive oil, sea salt, and, of course, Quentín's own line of coffees.

5. Taller Lu'um
Gabino Barreda 104,
colonia San Rafael

Taller Lu'um works with artisan communities from across Mexico to make unique modern pieces using traditional techniques. There is clothing and furniture but also vases, planters, dishware, and other smaller goods for the home and kitchen. It's appointment only, so make contact through their socials to visit the showroom.

6. Utilitario Mexicano
Marsella 3a,
colonia Juárez

The chic, minimalist items here are mostly geared toward the kitchen: copper and peltre (enameled steel) tableware, molcajetes, tortilla holders, manual juicers and grain mills, aprons, and a well-curated liquor selection.

BEYOND RESTAURANTS

Coffee Shops
Buna
Camino a Comala
Fuzz and Brew
Overeal

Bars
Fifty Mils
Handshake Speakeasy
Hanky Panky
Lazarus & Colin
    Meadery
Xaman Bar

Bakeries
Eminenta
Miga Café

Sweets
Casa Morgana
Joe Gelato
La Especial de París
La Rifa

VEGETARIAN AND VEGAN DINING

Around 20 percent of Mexicans are vegetarian or vegan, the most of any country in the Americas. So as much as Mexico City loves its meat tacos (see page 114) and seafood dishes (see page 157), it's not hard to cobble together a vegetarian meal at even the most carnivorous venues. Beside the inventive plant-centric dishes at upscale restaurants, many vegetarian visitors are surprised to find that even street food presents countless options: tlacoyos (page 43) of fava beans, pinto beans, and requesón (a ricotta-like cheese); quesadillas (see page 42) of squash blossoms, mushrooms, huitlacoche (see page 56), and rajas con queso (roast poblano chiles with cheese); tacos de guisado (see page 120) of cauliflower, eggplant, and nopales (cactus paddles). Mornings you can get tacos de canasta (see page 117) of potato or bean, and evenings a decadent cup of creamy esquites (see page 42).

Vegans—especially those who have struggled in other parts of Mexico—will be thrilled by the strength of Mexico City's vegan community. Here are ten favorite spots.

Alakazam

Guanajuato 54, colonia Roma Norte

This vegan Middle Eastern restaurant doubles as a terrific cocktail bar. Try an "Arakis Fremen" (arak, tequila, coconut water, lime, and butterfly pea tea) with your shawarma, lahmacun, fattoush, and all sorts of mezze.

Gatorta

Puebla 182, colonia Roma Norte

Fans of seitan, tofu, and other meat substitutes will get a kick out of Gatorta's overstuffed tacos al pastor (see page 120), tortas de milanesa (fried cutlets) with salsicha (tofu dogs), even "soyita pibil." Baked goods like donuts and cream-filled buns reiterate the comfort-food theme.

Gracias Madre

Tabasco 97, colonia Roma Norte

Some vegans may not be craving versions of popular taco fillings like tripas (intestines) and chicharrón (pork rinds), but judging by the perpetual lines here, there are plenty in CMDX who are craving them, as well as vegan tacos de suadero (see page 57), al pastor, chorizo (see page 55), and birria.

Malportaco
Diagonal San Antonio 1725, colonia Narvarte Oriente

The Malportaco folks spent more than a year developing not just their meat substitutes for common taco fillings (deeply flavorful and deliciously greasy) but a potato and coconut-based cheese that both melts and crisps, and salsas that are among the best in this salsa-crazed city. More importantly, they invented the "torta grosera," an over-the-top cheese-crusted torta stuffed with multiple tacos.

Mora Mora
Multiple locations, moramora.mx

There's something for everyone on the menu of vegan-restaurant classics here: juices, smoothies, salads, bowls (see opposite), and toasts. Your best bet, though, are the Mexican brunch dishes, like chilaquiles in chile morita sauce, mushroom carnitas, and garbanzo chorizo (see page 55).

Pali Pali
Oregon 751, colonia Del Valle Centro

Pali Pali's menu is a vegan survey of favorite antojitos (see page 53) and main dishes like pozole and chiles en nogada (stuffed poblano chiles in walnut sauce). Don't miss the fideo oaxaqueño, thin noodles cooked in a sauce of rare smoked pasilla mixe chile and dried avocado leaf, with a spicy bean sauce, avocado, and vegan queso fresco.

Plantasia
Puebla 120, colonia Roma Norte

Plantasia's pan-Asian dishes range from Nepalese momos to Indonesian mee goreng, from pad see ew to Peking "duck," all with a deep respect for traditional ingredients (where possible) and techniques.

Por Siempre Vegana
Manzanillo 18, colonia Roma Norte

Here you'll find vegan takes on taco fillings less seen at vegan taquerías: bistec encebollado ("beef" and onions), chicharrón en salsa verde ("pork" skin stewed in green sauce), and both green and red soy-based chorizo (see page 55).

Vegamo
Revillagigedo 47, colonia Centro

Don't miss the hearty breakfasts here, with dishes like "chicken" and waffles, red or green chilaquiles, enmoladas (enchiladas with mole sauce) stuffed with eggplant and corn, or the Jedi, a kind of vegan Grand Slam of egg, bacon, sausage, pancakes, and various vegetables and greens.

Veguísima
Pachuca 59, colonia Condesa

Burritos, being a northern dish, are few and far between in CDMX, which helps explain the popularity of Veguísima's enthusiastically overstuffed ones. Order yours "ahogado," sitting in a pool of mild red sauce.

SOUVENIRS

The best culinary souvenirs in Mexico City—edible and otherwise—aren't branded or mass-produced for export, so you'll want to stock up while you're here. Your local mercado (fixed-location food market), tianguis (temporary open-air market), and even street vendors are great places to start, and there are good one-stop-shopping craft markets like Mercado de Artesanías La Ciudadela and Coyoacán's Mercado Artesanal Mexicano. There are a few places where bargaining is expected—such as the sprawling antiques market Lagunilla—but if something has a price tag, don't bother.

KITCHEN AND HOME GOODS

Ceramics and Terra-cotta

When buying glazed terra-cotta cookware, be sure there's no lead in the glaze. Since there's no way to detect lead without a test kit (which you can purchase online), assume clay pots in neighborhood markets do contain lead, and buy only from vendors that explicitly advertise lead-free (libre de plomo), like the terrific Peregrinas in Mercado El 100 (page 20). Note that most Mexican ceramics are low-fired, which makes them more prone to breakage, so pack well. In addition to typical clay cookware, look for serving dishes made of Oaxaca's inky barro negro or Puebla's exuberant talavera styles, as well as pieces from modern ceramic artists you may stumble across.

Comal

The traditional low-fired clay comal (griddle) is likely to crack in your luggage, but they're affordable enough that it's worth buying a couple and packing well. And there's always a large selection of carbon steel and cast-iron comals in markets, which, for practical purposes, function as well or better than the clay ones. Larger food markets, like Mercado de la Merced (page 40) have the widest selection.

Copper

Mexico isn't the best place for heavy-duty copper cookware (since most copper pots here aren't lined, and copper reacts with acids), but for everything else—hand-forged copper trays, mixing bowls, utensil holders, napkin rings, Moscow Mule mugs, and much more—there are gorgeous versions at better markets and shops. Also look for the all-copper vendor at the La Ciudadela market (page 40).

Glassware

Fans of margaritas in giant blue-rimmed glasses will find plenty to love, but there are more interesting glasses and goblets in Mexico City, usually made of thick-walled glass that's likely to survive in your luggage. And when visiting larger places of worship, look for the clear glass votive-candle holders with a cross at the bottom, which double as traditional mezcal vessels.

Molcajetes

These volcanic stone mortars (the pestles are called manos or tejolotes, among other names) are heavy, but worth the effort of lugging home. Look for ones that are larger than you think you'll need (salsas have a way of splashing), with a relatively smooth finish. Larger food markets, like Mercado de la Merced (page 40), are the best places to look.

Molinillo

These intricately carved beaters used to froth hot chocolate will Mexicanize your kitchen in an instant, but look out—there are infinite variations in size, shape, and design, so collecting molinillos can become a lifelong addiction. Artefacto México in Escandón usually has an interesting selection.

Piloncillo Molds

The long wooden conical molds you might see at Lagunilla or other antiques markets? They're sugar molds (in which unrefined liquid sugar is poured to be dried for sale), and a cool addition to your kitchen, handy for holding nuts or dips, votive candles, or just for display.

Textiles

Mexico is a gold mine for table-cloths, runners, napkins, place mats, and coasters, and in Mexico City you can find quality examples from around the country. There's the wildly popular tenango embroidery of Hidalgo state, featuring rainbow-colored animals and landscapes, but also look for traditional Indigenous designs, from psychedelic Huichol to explosive Zapotec florals. Neighborhood food markets are a good place to stock up on things like dish towels and square cloths that are sized and shaped to fit in tortilla baskets; finer house-wares shops like Onora (page 89) and Metate (page 20) are best for tablecloths and matching sets of table linens.

Tortilla Tools

You don't need to come to Mexico to buy a simple tortilla press, but look for large, rustic wood and practical blue steel versions in almost every neighborhood market, and there are even high-end versions sold in specialty shops. Don't forget the woven or clay tortilla baskets, and cloth tortilla pouches.

EDIBLE

Chocolate

As a leading producer of chocolate, Mexico is a great source for everything from bulk chocolate to meticulously sourced chocolate bars and handmade confections. Any food market or specialty shop will have some range of chocolate treats, but also seek out beloved small producers like Oscuro Puro, Que Bo!, and La Rifa.

Coffee

Locally owned coffee shops usually use Mexican coffee beans (most Starbucks here even have an option from Chiapas), making a bag of fresh-roasted beans from your favorite local café a great souvenir. Just be sure to pick up a bottle of Licor 43 when you get home so you can make proper Mexican carajillos (espresso with the Spanish liqueur Licor 43, a common after-dinner treat).

Dried Chiles

Though dried chiles are widely available outside Mexico, they're often old and brittle (and sometimes mislabeled). Head to any neighborhood market to stock up on your favorites like ancho, guajillo, and morita, but also look for rarer ones like chilhuacle and the smoked Oaxacan pasilla mixe.

Honey

If you come across melipona honey—from a stingless bee in the Yucatán—grab it: It's incredibly flavorful but sold in small dropper bottles because it's more commonly used for medicinal than culinary purposes. But there are lots of other honeys available—often from single plants like coffee or mesquite—as well as a myriad of healthful bee products like propolis, pollen, and royal jelly. Many beekeepers sell their wares in the street, so don't be put off by roving vendors with carts of honey.

Jams

Even your local supermarket will have jams like guava, mango, and hibiscus, but check out specialty food markets and bakeries (like Rosetta Panadería) for small-batch jams, often with interesting herbs and spices added.

Mezcal and Other Spirits

These days, a good liquor store in any large US city has a better selection of artisanal mezcals than most shops in Mexico City, but some mezcalerías and mezcal-minded liquor stores—Mis Mezcales (page 20) and El Grifo (page 19) are two fantastic ones—may have mezcals not sold outside Mexico, even unbranded ones. Generally speaking, a traditionally made mezcal should have all the production info listed on the bottle (agave type, distiller's name and town, method of fermentation and distillation). Also look in liquor stores and farmers' markets for Mexican-made gins, whiskeys, and fruit liqueurs.

Mole Pastes

Any market—especially Oaxacan markets like Xaachila in Centro and Mercado Oaxaca in Escandón—will have an array of mole and pipián pastes (a pipián is, to overgeneralize, like a mole with a higher percentage of seeds or nuts than chiles). Once home, just add water or stock and you'll be instantly transported back. Beware: Though these pastes look dry and solid, they're usually counted as a "liquid" in your carry-on.

Salsas

The best souvenir is a salsa recipe (that's why you'll need the molcajete, page 73), but the quality of store-bought salsas is better than ever. Look in small gourmet-food shops like Distrito Foods (page 19) for the best examples. Salsa macha, which is primarily chiles and oil, is a powerful salsa with a long shelf life, and a little goes a long way, so it will serve as a tasty trip reminder for months to come.

Spices and Dried Herbs

Canela—Mexican cinnamon—is both larger and softer than the rock-hard and tightly rolled cinnamon sticks you may have grown up with. Look in neighborhood markets for large, loosely rolled sticks that can be eighteen inches or longer. Other dried herbs and spices hard to find outside Mexico are large Yucatecan allspice berries, Mexican oregano, dahlia roots and flowers, and various mints.

75

FOOD TOURS

Even if you're a seasoned traveler, even if you think you hate tours, if you plan to spend less than six months in Mexico City, taking a food tour is one of the best ways to ensure you don't get stuck in a tourist trap or miss all of the great context that makes each bite all the more meaningful. You'll also manage to taste some of the city's best street food while picking up some dining tips and tricks and an appreciation for the finer points of the city's dining culture.

Club Tengo Hambre
clubtengohambre.com

More of a collective of individual guides than one person's perspective, Club Tengo Hambre offers a variety of group and private tours. Along with the obligatory street food and Condesa outings, the company offers tours of Mercado de la Merced and "Mexico City After Dark," which are especially valuable for travelers that might be intimidated by the scope of both.

Devoured!
devoured.com.mx

Anaís Martinez, aka the Curious Mexican, runs these tours with six guides who each have their own areas of expertise. Look for her tours that go way off the beaten paths, and the "single serving sessions" that offer deep dives into a single topic like cacao, chiles, or fermentation.

Eat Like a Local
eatlikealocal.com.mx

Eat Like a Local's Rocío Sánchez is a strong believer in socially conscious tourism, and has created social programs for girls of families working in Mercado de la Merced. Her all-female team stresses personal connections with the cooks and vendors they visit and ensures that they only support businesses who maintain ethical working conditions.

Eat México

eatmexico.com

Eat México started in 2009, one of the first tour companies to prioritize the street food and informal mercados that tours at the time tended to gloss over. The team now continues to highlight under-the-radar vendors and neighborhoods, as in their popular "Narvarte at Night," which rambles through the underrated neighborhood's tacos, craft beer, and mezcal scenes.

Mexican Food Tours

mexicanfoodtours.com

With most tours offered multiple times daily, Mexican Food Tours is perfect if you're looking to book something on short notice. The tour of the historic San Ángel neighborhood is particularly interesting, folding in the area's deep cultural history along with delicious bites. They also offer several cooking classes.

Sabores México

saboresmexicofoodtours.com

Two unique tours that Sabores México offers are "Friends and Chocolate," a deep dive into Mexican chocolate with an experienced chocolatier, and an extensive food tour of Coyoacán (page 105) that goes behind the neighborhood's touristy facade.

Tyler's Taco Tours

instagram.com/tylers.taco.tours

Tyler's is a one-man operation and, as such, is a particularly intimate tour. Bilingual since age eight and a longtime Mexico City resident, he offers a unique binational perspective. Tyler focuses on the stories and people behind the tacos, with whom he has long-standing relationships, giving guests insight into the taqueros' everyday lives as well as their tacos.

Lomas de Chapultepec
Polanco
Santa Fe

POLANCO
DE CHAP

4

& LOMAS
ULTEPEC

POLANCO & LOMAS DE CHAPULTEPEC

AV. EJÉRCITO NACIONAL MEXICANO

CIRCUITO INTERIOR

AV. F. C. DE CUERNAVACA

DINING

1 Aitana
2 Aúna
3 Cantinetta del Becco
4 Carmela y Sal
5 Cascabel
6 Catamundi
7 Comedor Jacinta
8 Dante Brasa y Fuego
9 Eno
10 Guzina Oaxaca
11 Hunan
12 LagoAlgo
13 Malix
14 Los Panchos
15 Pujol
16 Quintonil
17 Restaurante El Cardenal Lomas
18 Siembra Comedor
19 Ticuchi
20 El Turix

SHOPPING

1 Aloisia Jardín de Té
2 Ingredienta
3 Lago
4 Onora
5 Tianguis de los Sábados Parque Lincoln
6 Tienda Rivero González

17

LOMAS DE CHAPULTEPEC

BLVD. DE LOS VIRREYES

11 3

5

SANTA FE ←

AV. RÍO SAN JOAQUÍN

BLVD. MIGUEL DE CERVANTES SAAVEDRA

POLANCO

AV. MOLIERE

C. ARQUIMIDES

AV. HOMERO

EJE 4

18

19
9

AV. HORACIO

2   **15**   **13**   **4**   **1**

AV. PDTE. MASARYK

20   **8**   **7**   **6**   **3**   **16**

5

6

AV. PASEO DE LA REFORMA

14 →

4
1

12

AV CONSTITUYENTES

POLANCO & LOMAS DE CHAPULTEPEC
DINING

The northwest side of Mexico City includes the cluster of Polanco, Lomas de Chapultepec, and Santa Fe neighborhoods, a wealthy residential and commercial bubble that houses some of Mexico City's best fine-dining restaurants, boutique and big-name hotels, museums, art galleries, and high-end shopping, all in the shadow of the biggest park of the metropolis: Chapultepec Park. Many visitors know Polanco mainly as the home of Pujol (page 86) and Quintonil (arguably the city's two most acclaimed restaurants), but the whole area is beautiful and worth recommending for reasons beyond its being "the fancy part of town."

Polanco's history dates back to the colonial era when Hernán Cortés gifted Moctezuma's first daughter—Doña Isabel de Moctezuma—the estate of Tacuba as a wedding present. By the mid-1600s, the estate had grown considerably in acreage and housed the Hacienda de San Juan de los Morales, a landholding dedicated to breeding silkworms. Throughout the centuries, the hacienda has been the private home and refuge to some of the most prominent families and personalities in the history of Mexico, and nowadays it operates as a restaurant and a private event space.

Lomas de Chapultepec is one of the most expensive neighborhoods in Mexico City. Planned and developed around the 1920s on the land that once belonged to the Hacienda de San Juan de los Morales, Lomas de Chapultepec was envisioned as the upscale housing zone for the Mexican nouveau rich families and up-and-coming business class in the aftermath of the Mexican Revolution. Today, Lomas de Chapultepec is still an enclave for Mexico City's wealthiest, where a mix of politicians, international dignitaries from numerous embassies, and the crème de la crème of Mexico's business class (including everyone's security detail) frequent a high-end dining scene that rewards those who dig for the substance beneath the style. Much of the area's architecture is in the Colonial Californiano style, a Mexican semi-baroque interpretation of the Spanish Colonial Revival, popular during Polanco's boom in the 1940s.

On the other hand, Santa Fe is Mexico City's corporate heart, and generally only business travelers end up there. It's an upscale commercial district of office buildings, chain hotels, malls, and expense-account restaurants, but also with many parks and family-oriented residential developments that make it a nice place to live, if not necessarily to visit (the hour-plus commute from any central neighborhood isn't very appealing). Still, there's plenty to do and eat if you find yourself there.

1. Aitana
Pedregal 24,
colonia Molino del Rey

Spain, Italy, and Mexico come together at chef Alberto Ituarte's breezy Lomas restaurant in a way that feels inspired rather than noncommittal. There are croquetas of jamón ibérico, house-made garganelli with a classic ragu, and rib-eye tacos, as well as mashups like a creamy saffron rice with grilled quail and an aioli of Oaxacan chile chihuacle. Where most restaurants that serve dinner in the city shut down around ten or eleven, Aitana—in true Spanish form—stays open daily until one A.M., making it one of the best late-night picks in the area.

2. Aúna
Anatole France 139,
colonia Polanco

This collaboration between Quintonil's Jorge Vallejo (page 86) and acclaimed young chef Fernando Torres was an instant hit upon opening at the end of 2023. It's split into a sunny all-day café on one side and a chic fine-dining restaurant on the other, where Torres serves colorful, vegetable-forward dishes like fried squash blossoms with mushroom cream, guava chutney, and salsa macha and raw kampachi with kale, mizuna, seaweed, and pumpkin-seed miso mayo.

3. Cantinetta del Becco
Sótano Torre 1, Avenida Javier Barros Sierra 540, Zedec Santa Fé

This Santa Fe restaurant offers superb Italian flavors, with most ingredients—olive oil, cheeses, charcuterie, and more—sourced directly from Italy. The wine list offers probably the biggest Italian selection in the city, with extensive grappa offerings as well. It's part of Grupo Becco, which, since 2002, has played a big part in raising the overall quality of Italian cooking in Mexico City.

4. Carmela y Sal
Torre Virreyes, Pedregal 24, colonia Molino del Rey

At the edge of the Lomas de Chapultepec corporate district, Carmela y Sal is a popular power-lunch destination that becomes more romantic at night, when the expense-account crowd has faded. Chef Gabriela Ruiz uses ingredients from her native state of Tabasco to create a playful menu that delicately incorporates tropical flavors and spices—think coconut prepared

as "chicharrón" in salsa verde, esquites (page 42) cooked risotto-style with Tabasqueño cream cheese, and bean-stuffed plantains under a shower of powdered pork (shown below).

5. Cascabel
Avenida Javier Barros Sierra 540, Zedec Santa Fé

Located in Santa Fe's Park Plaza, Cascabel is a cheery spot by chef Lula Martín del Campo with textbook versions of Mexico's homey culinary repertoire, like mole de olla (a soupy chile-based stew), frijol con puerco (pork and beans), and a range of antojitos (page 53) made from heirloom corn. Her reverence for traditional ingredients, techniques, and dishes is refreshing in a neighborhood that tends toward international and pan-Mediterranean cuisine.

6. Catamundi
Alejandro Dumas 97, colonia Polanco

Catamundi is a wine and gourmet-food shop, restaurant, and bakery just off Parque Lincoln, a good choice for an easy-breezy meal at any time of day, with a good list of wines by the glass as well as cocktails. Start the day here with an invigorating smoothie of passion fruit, turmeric, and banana and a dish of egg whites in salsa verde with fava beans.

7. Comedor Jacinta
Virgilio 40, colonia Polanco

Chef Edgar Núñez (of Sud 777 fame, page 110) opened this casual Polanco spot as a neighborhood fonda featuring the homey dishes of his mother, aunt, and grandmother. The typical family fonda (see page 56), though, doesn't feature such carefully sourced ingredients

or have a Michelin-starred chef in the kitchen. Beef tongue comes with purslane, beans, and smoked chile, bone marrow tacos are brightened by lamb's quarters (greens), and his chamorro (pork shank)—a cantina favorite—comes in a pasilla sauce enriched with pulque. Even the lentil soup tastes special. The drink menu revolves around an extensive tequila selection, with margaritas in ten flavors that include avocado and lemon verbena.

8. Dante Brasa y Fuego
Edgar Allan Poe 41,
colonia Polanco

Argentinian chef Dante Ferrero's casual restaurant in Polanco focuses on the Argentinian tradition of asado (grilling) using aged, high-quality meat. Portions of its perfectly grilled beef cuts are generous; try the asado de tira (short rib), Wagyu rib eye, or dry-aged New York steak along with less-traditional sides like grilled Brussels sprouts, queso fundido with housemade beef chorizo, smoked burrata, and goat empanadas. There are also Mexican dishes like tacos, ceviche, and barbacoa (see page 116. This is a must in Polanco for carnivores.

9. Eno
Petrarca 258,
colonia Polanco

Eno is famed chef Enrique Olvera's all-day café, especially good for breakfast and lunch. Eno has two locations in Polanco—on Petrarca Street and inside the contemporary art museum, Jumex. Both options are cute venues to hang out in the afternoon and try exceptional versions of favorites like esquites (page 55) and torta de milanesa (pork cutlet sandwich).

10. Guzina Oaxaca
Avenida Presidente Masaryk 513,
colonia Polanco

Renowned Oaxacan chef Alejandro Ruiz brings a taste of his hometown to Mexico City at Guzina Oaxaca, consistently one of the city's best options for upscale Oaxacan. The restaurant specializes in classics like a black mole from the Mixteca region, plantain molotes (fried stuffed masa fritters), Oaxaca-style barbacoa (see page 116), and antojitos (see page 53) straight from the comal. Guzina

Oaxaca is also a good option for breakfast before a day of Polanco shopping.

11. Hunan
Avenida Paseo
de la Reforma 2210,
colonia Lomas de Virreyes

Hunan offers a high-end Mexicanized interpretation of Chinese food whose popularity has spawned many imitators since it opened in 1993. Classic decoration, formal old-school service, and delicious food are the selling points. Order the restaurant's classics like Hunan lamb and Return of the Phoenix (the sesame chicken of your dreams), but don't miss the tacos de arrachera, an off-menu delight grilled on the teppan (think Benihana), which can stand toe-to-toe with any taquería.

12. LagoAlgo
Bosque de Chapultepec,
Pista El Sope s/n,
colonia Bosque de Chapultepec II

Overlooking one of the lakes in Chapultepec Park, LagoAlgo is both an art gallery and a restaurant committed to free-range meat, sustainable seafood, and organic produce from local farms. The space, designed as part of Mexico's urban development projects surrounding the 1968 Olympics, features stunning Brutalist architecture and a charming view from the dining room. For many

85

15. Pujol

Tennyson 133,
colonia Polanco

Star chef Enrique Olvera's signature restaurant is Pujol. Founded in 2000, the restaurant's tasting menu and, more recently, the bar's "taco omakase" have captivated local and international palates with iconic dishes like the Mole Madre—a combination of long-aged and freshly made moles plated one atop the other—and baby corn covered in chicatana ant mayonnaise. Olvera's cooking style interprets ancient Mexican culinary traditions based on heirloom corn and the milpa—the country's unique agricultural system—through a modern lens. After more than two decades, Pujol remains among the best places to dine in all of Mexico and consistently ranks high among the best in Latin America and beyond.

16. Quintonil

Avenida Isaac Newton 55,
colonia Polanco

Chef Jorge Vallejo and his wife, Alejandra Flores, deliver one of the city's best culinary experiences at Quintonil. Along with Pujol, it's not just ranked as one of Mexico's best on every reputable fine-dining list, but among the world's best due to its creativity in capturing Mexico's seasonal ingredients and local flavors.

decades, the grand building housed different restaurant projects and concepts, but after the pandemic, this dual art and culinary project gave new life to a somehow forgotten dining destination. Pin this one for dinner with a view.

13. Malix

Avenida Isaac Newton 104,
colonia Polanco

Chef Alonso Madrigal worked at local hot spots such as as Rosetta, Em, and Loup Bar before opening his first restaurant. Malix is small yet well-designed and welcoming, a modest backdrop for creative dishes like beef sweetbreads with nettle chimichurri, duck breast with mole and carrots, and guacamole with trout roe and salt-cured cactus.

14. Los Panchos

Tolstoi 9,
colonia Anzures

With more than seventy-five years of preparing some of the best carnitas in Mexico City, Los Panchos is a family-run restaurant focused on traditional Mexican dining. Besides carnitas, Los Panchos also offers lamb barbacoa (see page 116), and both dishes can be ordered as a taco or by the pound. Order enough sides of guacamole, pico de gallo, and chicharrones (pork rinds) to top each taco on your table. The ambiance is family-friendly, with a taquero also stationed outside if you need to grab tacos on the run.

The roots of Vallejo's tasting menus are traditional and unpretentious—various moles, pipiánes (seed-based sauces), antojitos (see page 53), barbacoa, and the like—but all with personal twists and impeccably sourced ingredients. Quintonil also features one of Mexico's best wine lists, and tasting menu pairings are reliably eye-opening.

17. Restaurante El Cardenal Lomas

Avenida Paseo de las Palmas 215, colonia Lomas de Chapultepec

When this location of the city's historic El Cardenal restaurant chain opened in 2006, it was its first outside the Centro Histórico, with a modern design that seemed at odds with the very traditional fare. It has turned out to be one of the chain's most popular locations, appealing to an upscale crowd that craves its famously hearty, unpretentious food. While El

Cardenal is often recommended for breakfast, this is an elegant place to end a busy day of sightseeing in a neighborhood you might not otherwise visit.

18. Siembra Comedor

Avenida Ejército Nacional Mexicano 314, colonia Polanco

After a couple of years focused on sourcing heirloom corn from local producers with sustainable practices for a tortilla shop and a small taquería, Siembra Comedor is now a casual restaurant with an extensive menu where several Mexican corn varieties shine through in corn-centric preparations like tostadas, tlacoyos (see page 43), tacos, and gorditas. Try dishes like fish pastor taco, the pork rind gordita, and the chocolate tamal with cacao nibs.

19. Ticuchi

Petrarca 254, colonia Polanco

The swankiest place to drink mezcal in Polanco is Ticuchi. The candlelit interior mixes concrete, wood, and velvet finishes for a supper-club vibe with a 360-degree bar at the center. The extremely well-curated list of agave spirits is a draw, but—as expected in a place owned by chef Enrique Olvera—the Oaxacan-inspired menu of mostly vegetarian, mostly small plates is impeccable.

Try any of the antojitos (see page 53) or tamales, and, if available, the tlayuda made with peanut "asiento" (normally pork lard) and fish "tasajo" (normally dried beef).

20. El Turix

Avenida Emilio Castelar 212, colonia Polanco

Street food and small-scale eateries or taquerías are hard to come by in Polanco, since the neighborhood caters heavily to high-end diners. However, certain casual options have gained a foothold, such as El Turix, a local joint famous for its cochinita pibil—a Yucatecan dish of shredded pork in a marinade of achiote and spices. Order your cochinita in tacos, on panuchos (fried bean-stuffed tortillas), or in tortas (sandwiches), and pile on plenty of pickled onions and a dash of habanero salsa to cut the richness. Turix's extra-saucy version may lack some of the complexity of great Yucatecan cochinita pibil, which is cooked in an earthen pit with banana leaves, but it's exceptional comfort food. Several other locations have opened—including two in nearby Lomas de Chapultepec—but this is the original, and a great Polanco option when time and/or wallet don't allow for a more lavish experience.

87

POLANCO & LOMAS DE CHAPULTEPEC
SHOPPING

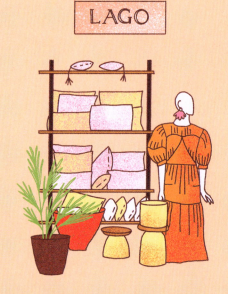

LAGO

Being the "fancy" part of town, there's plenty of shopping to be had in Polanco, even if much of it is international luxury chains and large-scale malls. It's a beautiful area to walk around in, though, so besides the places below, just walk along the main drags of Campos Elíseos and Masaryk, where there are new shops opening constantly.

1. Aloisia Jardín de Té
Euler 152-Interior 305, colonia Polanco
Aloisia is a Mexican tea brand, which makes complex combinations of globally and locally sourced teas and other plants, with nods to Mexican herbalism and gastronomy. Grab a seat by the curved floor-to-ceiling windows and explore creations like Tribu de Brujas (Witches' Tribe), a blend of pu'erh tea with Aztec marigold, calendula, cacao, mint, and chamomile.

2. Ingredienta
Avenida Homero 1500 Local 2A, colonia Polanco
Ingredienta is a local gourmet convenience store with outposts in Polanco, Lomas de Chapultepec, and Pedregal. It is an excellent source for upscale ingredients and local marmalades, sauces, spices, chocolate, and organic produce. Come here for gastro-souvenirs, gifts for local friends, or to stock the fridge where you're staying.

3. Lago
Avenida Presidente Masaryk 310, colonia Polanco
From the outside, Lago may look like one of the many lovely upscale boutiques in the neighborhood. Don't pass it by, though, as the shop highlights Mexican designers in all fields, including ceramics and kitchenware that are often exclusive to Lago. Get on its online mailing list to be notified of the many pop-up markets and events hosted here.

4. Onora
Lope de Vega 330, colonia Polanco
Onora is arguably the best store in the city for kitchen and home decor. While the goods in Mexico City's craft markets can be frustratingly similar, as if they're all buying from the same suppliers, here you'll find unique ceramics, textiles, and other handmade pieces from the country's best artisans. Much of the work is collaborations between Onora and traditional artists that straddle tradition and modern design.

5. Tianguis de los Sábados Parque Lincoln
Parque Lincoln, colonia Polanco
On Saturday mornings, Polanco's lovely Parque Lincoln turns into an open-air food market that, like most tianguis (transient weekly markets), is equal parts shopping and eating. Fitting the upscale neighborhood, both quality and selection are top-notch; grab a tepache (page 57) or michelada to stroll with and try bites from as many stands as you can muster.

6. Tienda Rivero González
Julio Verne 39, colonia Polanco
This retail outpost of a terrific winery in Coahuila state is a good place to buy wine to take home, while learning a bit about Mexican wine in general from the friendly staff. The shop also stocks products from its farms, like soft and sweet pecans, olive oil, honey, and various fruit compotes.

BEYOND RESTAURANTS

Coffee Shops
La Caja de Cristal
Catamundi
Chiquitito Café
Cucurucho Polanco
Mallorca

Bars
Gin Gin Polanco
Ley Zanahoria
Limantour Polanco
Living Room Bar
Mulligan's

Bakeries
Caffé Biscottino
La Conchería
Fougasse
Mätre
Niddo
Odette

Sweets
El Cafeto
Culto Cacaotería
Dulcería El Secreto
Que Bo!

A PERFECT TWENTY-FOUR HOURS (AND THEN SOME) IN MEXICO CITY

By Alonso Ruvalcaba

9:00 A.M.

Skip the perpetual line at chef Elena Reygadas's bakery Rosetta Panadería, and reserve a table at her sunny all-day café **Lardo**, where you can still get her signature rollo de guayaba (guava pastry) along with heartier fare like eggs with cascabel chile and the anisey herb hoja santa, or chilaquiles in salsa verde with seared nopales (cactus paddles) and a ball of burrata oozing over the top. If possible, save some room and take a scenic stroll through Condesa's two iconic neighboring parks—Parque España and Parque México—en route to a folding table on the southeast corner of Aguascalientes and Chilpancingo. Here, "El Don" has been serving tacos de canasta (see page 117) since 1986; try potato or chicharrón (pork rinds).

Lardo
Agustín Melgar 6, colonia Condesa

Tacos de Canasta "El Don"
Aguascalientes and Chilpancingo (corner), colonia Condesa

11:00 A.M.

Crossing over from Condesa into Roma, you'll find **Mercado Medellín** in full swing by late morning. It's as vital as any of the city's 329 covered public markets, but is all the more important in colonia Roma as the neighborhood's rapid gentrification keeps pushing out long-standing traditional businesses. Mercado Medellín is known for its large selection of South American and Caribbean products—things from Colombia, Peru, Venezuela, Cuba, and even hard-to-find ingredients from Yucatán—as well as all the produce, butchers, fishmongers, cookware, and food stands you'll find at any good neighborhood market. For a snack, try the Cuban food at **Sazón del Mongo**, or carnitas tacos at **Meche y Rafael**.

Mercado Medellín
Campeche 101, colonia Roma Sur

1:00 P.M.

Take a ten-minute car ride to Don Ricardo's blue truck parked near the busy intersection of Luz Saviñon and Universidad, where, under the name **Tacos Richard**, he serves tacos de guisado (see page 120) from the trunk with the brisk banter of a seasoned bartender. The dozen or so fillings change daily, but you can usually count on chicharrón prensado (a kind of pork cake), costillas (pork ribs) en salsa verde, bistec (steak) a la mexicana, and potatoes in roast poblano chile and cream. Narvarte is arguably the best taco neighborhood in the city, so if Ricardo isn't there (he usually takes Tuesdays, Thursdays, and most weekends off), you'll find several great options within a block: **La Taquiza al Carbón**, **El Fénix**, **Don Frank**, **Tacos Tony**, and **El Vilsito**. The latter you especially want to keep in mind for later since it's open

until three A.M. (five A.M. on weekends). If you feel you've earned a beer by now, stroll up Cumbres de Maltrata street to **Cerveza en Punto**, a shop and taproom where the servers will educate you all about Mexican craft beer.

Tacos Richard
Petén 227, colonia Narvarte

Cerveza en Punto
La Morena 908, colonia Narvarte

3:00 P.M.

If the Centro Histórico is the belly of the city, then Calle López is its large intestine. There's something for everyone on this eight-block stretch on the western edge of the Centro: flautas poblanas at **La Olla de la Abundancia**, green chorizo tacos at **Ricos Tacos Toluca**, the whole-pig cochinita pibil at **El Taco de Oro de la XEW**, stewed beef kidneys at **Cocina Mi Fonda**. Mercado San

Juan will be starting to close down, but **El Mercadito Peruano**, a market stand that happens to double as one of the best Peruvian restaurants in the city, is open until five. Enjoy the neighborhood until the sun goes down by shopping at **Mercado de Artesanías La Ciudadela** (page 40), ducking into the museums Museo de Arte Popular or Museo Memoria y Tolerancia, or just having a coffee at **Finca Don Porfirio** (page 35), a café on the eighth floor of Sears with the best view of Palacio de Bellas Artes.

La Olla de la Abundancia
Mercado de San Juan Arcos de Belén, local 310
Av Arcos de Belén 41, Centro Histórico

Ricos Tacos Toluca
López 103, Centro Histórico

El Taco de Oro de la XEW
López 107, Centro Histórico

Cocina Mi Fonda
López 101, Centro Histórico

El Mercadito Peruano
Segunda Calle de Ernesto Pugibet s/n-Local 279, Centro Histórico

7:00 P.M.

Now that you've made it to cocktail hour, grab an Ecobici (rental bike stations located all over town) and ride west along Paseo de la Reforma, the city's most important avenue, and where citywide protests and celebrations alike often gather. Take a right at the iconic El Ángel de la Independencia monument commemorating Mexico's independence and find yourself in colonia Cuauhtémoc's "Little Japan." **Tokyo Music Bar** is modeled, obviously, after Tokyo listening bars, and is one of the city's most elegant bars, decked out in emerald and gold with ornate parquet flooring. The drinks, however, have locally sourced ingredients like guava, cedrón (Mexican lemon balm), chamomile, and chiles. Wine fans can head downstairs to the same owners' **Le Tachinomi Desu**, a discreet standing-only natural wine bar that's a popular hangout for restaurant and bar industry workers.

Tokyo Music Bar
Río Pánuco 132, colonia Cuauhtémoc

Le Tachinomi Desu
Río Pánuco 132-1a, colonia Cuauhtémoc

9:00 P.M.

Even though many cantinas are closed at night, their concept—booze and drink-friendly food that can span snacks to full meals—is a good one in a city where the main meal is a late lunch. **Salón Ríos** has an old-school cantina spirit but with a modern food and drink sensibility and sharp design (and, unlike historic cantinas that close by nine, it's open most nights until two A.M.). Try a marlin-stuffed chile relleno taco, or chamorro (pork shank) in manchamanteles (a fruity Oaxacan mole) with Mexican wines by the glass or more than two dozen mezcals in generous two-ounce pours. Alternatively, head to **Wanwan Sakaba** (page 67), whose izakaya concept is basically a Japanese cantina, for all sorts of traditional raw and cooked dishes with sake, shochu, and Japanese whisky.

Salón Ríos
Río Nilo 71, colonia Cuauhtémoc

Wanwan Sakaba
Londres 209, colonia Juárez

11:00 P.M.

Colonia Juárez is a sort of mixology mecca, with hotspots like **Hanky Panky**, **Handshake Speakeasy**, **Xaman**, **Long Story Short**, **The Brooklyn Rippers**, **Cicatriz Café** (page 64), and even great hotel bars like **Fifty Mils** in the Four Seasons and the **King Cole Bar** at the St. Regis. Mexico's cocktail scene has been gaining international attention for its mix of classic cocktail artistry with Mexican spirits (not just tequila and mezcal but Mexican gins, rums, and whiskeys), ferments like pulque (see page 51), tepache (see page 57), and hidromiel (mead), and various herbs, seeds, flowers, and insects in addition to Mexican fruits and vegetables. Most bars offer snacks with the same nods to tradition.

Hanky Panky
Turín 52, colonia Juárez

Handshake Speakeasy
Calle Amberes 65, colonia Juárez

Xaman
Copenhague 6, colonia Juárez

Long Story Short
Florencia 51-Local B2, colonia Juárez

The Brooklyn Rippers
Liverpool 10, colonia Juárez

Fifty Mils
Avenida Paseo de la Reforma 439, colonia Juárez

King Cole Bar
Avenida Paseo de la Reforma 439, colonia Cuauhtémoc

1:00 A.M.

Need a late-night snack? Well, you haven't had tacos al pastor yet (and you can't leave Mexico City without eating tacos al pastor), so hit up **Tacos Don Güero**. The place never closes, so you can make it breakfast instead, if that's how you roll. Don't stop at pastor, though; try a torta of

suadero (see page 57) with longaniza, or a steak gringa (on a flour
tortilla with cheese). Wash it down
with agua de jamaica (hibiscus) or
horchata (sweetened rice).

Tacos Don Güero
Río Nilo 66, colonia Cuauhtémoc

7:00 A.M.
Mercado de la Merced (page 40)
opens at five thirty A.M., and by seven
most vendors are caffeinated and
wisecracking while other neighborhood markets are barely waking
up. The largest market in the city
(and, no doubt, one of the largest
covered daily markets in the world),
Merced (or "La Meche," if you want
to sound chilango) is a microcosm of
the city. Virtually everything locals
eat, drink, buy, and sell can be found
here. The guys walking around with
candy-rimmed plastic cups? It's not
your imagination: Those are indeed
micheladas (like fishermen, market
workers keep atypical hours). Join
in, especially if you want to peruse
the live animals and other ritualistic
accoutrements at **Mercado Sonora**
(page 41) next door.

9:00 A.M.
Get to know a part of the Centro
Histórico that most tourists miss.
The pedestrian-only Talavera street
is Baby Jesus Lane, with everything

you need to dress up your Niño Dios
doll in elaborate finery year-round.
Walking north, Talavera becomes
Alhóndiga, with a concentration of
beauty supply shops, and then, still
walking north, it's renamed De La
Santísima, a block-long mini Oaxaca
with several shops selling Oaxacan
ingredients and crafts (don't miss
the bargain-priced burnished clay
tableware at **Oaxaca en Mexico**).
Your morning snack isn't Oaxacan,
though, but all the taco-adjacent
antojitos (see page 53) waiting
just through the narrow stone door-
way at **Antojitos Esther**: fava-bean
tlacoyos (page 53), chicharrón
(pork rind) gorditas (see page 42),
huitlacoche quesadillas (see page
56), and sopes (see page 42)
topped with shredded beef or maybe
the more breakfast-y eggs and
mushrooms.

Oaxaca en Mexico
De La Santísima 16, Centro Histórico

Antojitos Esther
De La Santísima 22, Centro Histórico

11:00 a.m.
Pay respects at Templo de la
Santísima Trinidad, a glorious
Spanish baroque church whose
construction started in 1580 but has
been through several restorations,
due to its sinking into the lake bed
it (and all of the Centro) is built on.

From here, two options: Market fans will check out the Mercado Abelardo L. Rodríguez, built in 1934 as one of the city's first covered neighborhood markets and a prototype for the ones to follow. The architecture is a stately mix of baroque, art nouveau, and art deco, with several murals painted by Diego Rivera's students and colleagues. Order huesitos at Carnitas Michoacanas "Don One," pork ribs and neck chops boiled in lard and eaten with your hands.

Or, if you haven't yet been to the Zócalo (said to be the world's second-largest public plaza next to Tiananmen Square), visit the Catedral Metropolitana and the Templo Mayor, and keep the historic theme going with a tequila at **Cantina la Potosina**, a cantina that's remained largely unchanged since it opened in 1890.

Templo de la Santísima Trinidad
Emiliano Zapata 60, Centro Histórico

Mercado Abelardo L. Rodríguez, Centro
República de Venezuela 72, Centro Histórico

Carnitas Michoacanas "Don One"
República de Venezuela 72, Centro Histórico

Cantina la Potosina
Jesús María 21, Centro Histórico

1:30 P.M.
Escape to the south, where the gorgeous and historic neighborhoods

of San Ángel and Coyoacán are a short drive away (though traffic in and out of the Centro is no fun) but feel almost like the separate towns that they once were before the metropolis swallowed them up. **San Ángel Inn** (page 110), across the street from Diego Rivera's studio, is a former hacienda–turned–luxury restaurant. Tell them you're just there for drinks and want to sit in the passageways around the courtyard, for maximum people-watching and to chat with the roving mariachis between songs. Order immaculate martinis and margaritas with duck tacos, a tableside Caesar, and escamoles (aka Mexican caviar) to share. If it's Saturday, walk to **El Bazaar Sábado**, an indoor design market that's expanded in a three-block radius in every direction with all things art, design, antique, and edible. If it's not Saturday, head to Coyoacán's Jardín Centenario for a stroll in the park and for coffee at **Café Avellaneda**, a mezcal flight at **Mezcalero Coyoacán**, or tacos of wild boar or venison at **La Casa de los Tacos**.

El Bazar Sábado
Plaza San Jacinto 11, colonia San Ángel

Café Avellaneda
Higuera 40-A, colonia La Concepción

Mezcalero Coyoacán
Caballocalco 14, colonia La Concepción

La Casa de los Tacos
Felipe Carrillo Puerto 16, colonia Villa Coyoacán

5:30 P.M.

Take a scenic ride to Polanco for a preprandial drink at Enrique Olvera's **Ticuchi**, located in Pujol's (page 86) original location. Try a Nosferatu, a Negroni riff with mezcal and the southern Mexican herb rosita de cacao (which isn't actually cacao), and close with a palate cleanser of mezcal-and-melon sorbet with the Oaxacan smoked pasilla mixe chile.

Ticuchi
Petrarcha 254, colonia Polanco

7:00 P.M.

Assuming you made your reservation months ago, the evening ends with a leisurely tasting menu at **Quintonil** (page 86), one of the restaurants that defines modern Mexico City fine dining. Choose the Chef's Menu (usually around twelve courses, a bit more elaborate than the Seasonal Menu), with an optional beverage pairing of all Mexican wines. Groups of four or less can book the Barra, facing the open kitchen, for an even more intimate experience.

ALL-NIGHT EATING

Bars in Mexico City can serve until two thirty A.M., and there are plenty of taquerías to cater to their clientele. Favorites like **El Vilsito** (page 135), **Tacos el Buen Tono** (page 153), **Tacos "Beto"** (page <?>), **Tacos Manolo** (page 135), and the popular **El Califa** chain are open at least until three A.M. on weekends, but there are great 24/7 picks that are good not only for late night but for grabbing a bite before an early-morning day trip or flight.

Au Pied de Cochon
Campos Elíseos 218, colonia Polanco
The French onion soup is a must at this luxe branch of a Paris icon from the 1940s (page 142).

Birria de Don Chuy
Violeta 30, colonia Guerrero
Any birria tastes good when you're hungry and desperate at four A.M., but it helps that Don Chuy's is among the best in town.

El Borrego Viudo
Avenida Revolución 241, colonia Tacubaya
Its name means "the widowed sheep," but there's no lamb here; instead order tacos al pastor (see page 120) and cachete (beef cheek).

Café el Popular
Avenida 5 de Mayo 50 y 52, colonia Centro
Just a block from the Zócalo, the large, something-for-everything menu at this sit-down spot is a great Centro choice at any hour.

La Casa de Toño
Avenida Cuauhtémoc 439,
colonia Piedad Navarte

This branch of a popular chain (page 150) is just a block south of Roma Sur and less than fifteen minutes from the airport in the early morning. Breakfast is served all day, but it's hard to resist the pozole or flautas ahogadas.

Churrería El Moro
Eje Central Lázaro Cárdenas 42,
colonia Centro

Since churros are equally apt as breakfast, dessert, or just a bready booze sponge, it's nice to have the city's best available anytime (page 35).

Los Cocuyos
Simón Bolívar 59, colonia Centro

This classic place for tacos de fritanga (see page 119) has cheerful (if inebriated) crowds at all hours.

Deigo Ramen
Multiple locations,
deigoramen.com.mx

All three Deigo locations are open 24/7, making for a truly unexpected late-night meal or early breakfast. Choose from nine ramen types, plus takoyaki, gyoza, and edamame, in cozy locales meant to mimic Japanese ramen houses, from the long-simmered broths and noodles handmade daily, to the taps of free green tea and the high-tech automated bathroom.

Juguería Caro
Avenida Sonora 209, colonia Condesa

This all-natural juice stand is less for late-nighters and more for the very-early-morning crowd: swing-shifters, early-morning joggers, and insomniacs.

Ojo de Agua
Clave 444, colonia Vallejo Poniente

Choose from healthy-ish juices and salads or traditional Mexican antojitos (see page 53) at this longtime favorite north of Centro (page 150).

Súper Tacos Chupacabras
Avenida Río Churubusco 13,
colonia Del Carmen

Most of the Coyoacán late-nighters here are ordering the "chupacabras" taco, a mix of steak, chorizo (see page 55), and cecina (partially dried beef), with piles of optional garnishes.

Tacos Don Güero
Río Nilo 66, colonia Cuauhtémoc

Simple meat tacos are the draw here, with or without cheese (tread carefully, as they're generous to a fault with the cheese).

Tortas al Fuego
Avenida Sonora 205, colonia Condesa

The tortas are terrific here, plus there are chilaquiles and egg dishes if you're craving a very early breakfast.

SPOTLIGHT: JAPANESE FOOD

First-time (and, for that matter, second- or third-time) visitors to Mexico City are often struck by the proliferation of Japanese and Japanese-inspired restaurants, shops, and groceries. There are more than one hundred local Japanese restaurants on OpenTable alone, which doesn't take into account the hundreds more informal noodle and sando shops, street carts serving sushi, tempura, yakitori, kushiage, okonomiyaki, and rice dishes, and Japanese-inspired coffee, tea, whisky, and cocktail bars. Many non-Japanese restaurants serve Nami, a sake made in the traditional method in Sinaloa state, and even Pujol (page 86) offers a "taco omakase" tasting menu. What's the deal?

There's a long history of Japanese immigration to Mexico, starting with Japanese slaves brought on the galleon trade that ran between Manila and Acapulco from 1565 to 1815. Mexico was the first Latin American country to officially welcome Japanese immigrants in 1897, who mostly came to work on coffee and sugar plantations and in coal mines. During World War II, after Mexico formally declared war against the Axis Powers (including Japan) in 1942, the government required all Japanese immigrants to move away from borders and coastal areas. More than 80 percent moved to Mexico City, where employment was allowed and there was an existing Japanese community as well as a Japanese language school. Most stayed in the city after the war.

The jacaranda trees that are a hallmark of early spring, when they explode in puffy purple florescence, are a legacy of Japanese immigration.

Tatsugoro Matsumoto was an imperial gardener from Tokyo who moved to Mexico City in 1896 after working on the Japanese Tea Garden in San Francisco's Golden Gate Park for the 1894 World's Fair. In the early 1930s, Mexico's president, Pascual Ortiz Rubio, wanted to honor diplomatic relations with Japan by covering the city in thousands of cherry trees; Matsumoto, who owned a nursery at the time, thought jacarandas were more suited for the climate. He went on to oversee planting of many of the bougainvillea and non-native palm trees that are also so embedded in the cityscape.

CDMX is a city that loves both seafood and noodles (usually called fideos when angel-hair thin, and tallarines when thicker), so Japanese food has long had a foothold in chilango hearts. However, one restaurant group has been largely responsible for Mexico City's Japanese food scene garnering international attention. Led by Edo López, a Tijuana native of Japanese heritage, the Edo Kobayashi group opened Rokai in 2013, with Japanese chef Hiroshi Kawahito offering sushi omakase—immaculately sourced from both Mexico and Japan—in an understatedly chic room. They now have eleven restaurant concepts and three bars across the city (with more throughout Mexico and the United States), have created a sort of "Little Tokyo" in colonia Cuauhtémoc north of the Japanese embassy, and in the process have established a new baseline of quality and legitimacy for Japanese cooking in the region.

Another Mexican with Japanese heritage with an outsized impact on the CDMX culinary scene is Eduardo Nakatani, whose grandfather invented the ubiquitous snack cacahuates japoneses (Japanese peanuts), peanuts roasted in a brittle wheat-flour shell. As a chef, consultant, and educator, Nakatani has done much to promote authentic Japanese cooking, while finding common foodways between the two countries' cuisines. He now teaches classes on ramen and owns the bustling Fideo Gordo, which specializes in kishimen (thick flat udon), in both traditional preparations with Mexican chiles and riffs on birria and barbacoa (see page 116). The restaurant is the perfect place to experience the ways Japanese cuisine and culture have been seamlessly—if unexpectedly—integrated into the Mexico City landscape.

Fideo Gordo
Salamanca 87, colonia Roma Norte
This inventive Japanese noodle house specializes in kishimen, with some Mexican touches.

Kaito Izakaya

J. Enrique Pestalozzi 1238,
colonia Del Valle Centro

This bar is all about fun snacks—takoyaki (octopus balls), chapulín (grasshopper) maki—and signature cocktails that combine sake with mezcal, tequila, and gin.

Kameyama Shachu

Avenida Álvaro Obregón 230-Local A,
colonia Roma Norte

The only Latin American retailer of Osaka's Sakai Takayuki brand of hand-forged knives.

Kill Bill

Orizaba 39, colonia Roma Norte

At this stylish fourteen-seat self-described "hi-fi, sushi, and robata bar," diners can choose from three omakase menus, one with all Mexican fish and all with a mix of nigiri sushi and robata (grilled) items.

Kura

Colima 378-Local A, colonia Roma Norte

This authentic izakaya (a Japanese cantina, if you will) has extensive food and drink menus and an often boisterous crowd (page 14).

Raku Café

Sinaloa 188, colonia Roma Norte

Come to this cute coffee shop for serious coffee and traditional matcha, with sandos made on real shokupan (Japanese sandwich bread).

Ryo Kan

Río Pánuco 166, colonia Cuauhtémoc

Deeply Japanese in both its design and its hospitality, this hotel's ten suites here are contemporary riffs on traditional Kyoto residences. Non-guests can book day passes that include a traditional tea ceremony and use of the rooftop baths.

Sakenaya James

Avenida Chapultepec 482A,
colonia Roma Norte

This Japanese-owned fish market specializes in bluefin tuna that's broken down in-house, as well as a range of sashimi-quality seafood. It doubles as a tiny restaurant serving raw and cooked small bites.

Súper Mikasa

San Luis Potosí 173, colonia Roma Norte

There are many Japanese groceries in Mexico City, but this workhorse of a shop usually has the best assortment of fresh and pantry items, along with premade food and housewares.

Sushi Kyo

Havre 77, colonia Juárez

This is arguably the best—and one of the most intimate—Edomae-style omakase experiences in town, with fish sourced from both Mexico and Japan.

Agrícola
Del Carmen
El Rosario
Guadalupe Inn
Jardines del Pedregal
San Ángel
San Ángel Inn
Tizapán San Ángel
Villa Coyoacán

COYOAC
ÁNGEL & I

5

ĀN, SAN
NVIRONS

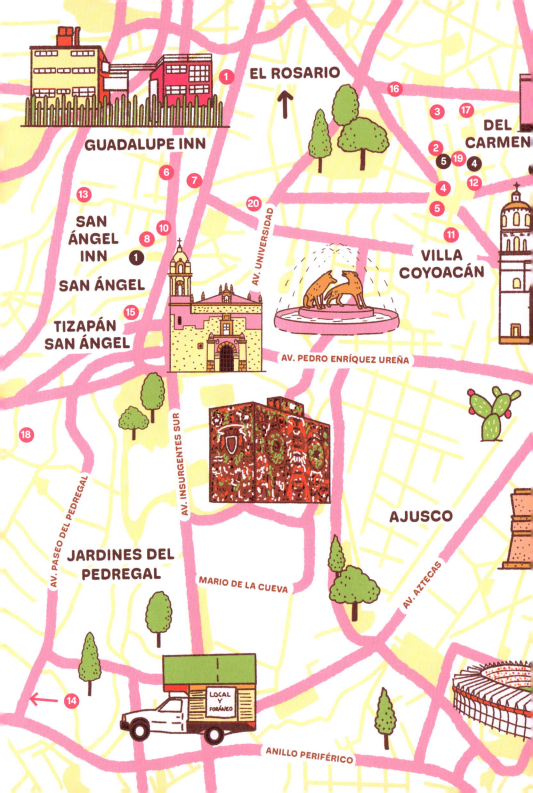

AGRÍCOLA

AV. RÍO CHURUBUSCO

TLALPAN

COYOACÁN, SAN ÁNGEL & ENVIRONS

DINING

1 Los Almendros
2 La Barraca Valenciana
3 Chamorros Coyoacán
4 Corazón de Maguey
5 Los Danzantes
6 Eloise Chic Cuisine
7 Guadiana
8 La Jacinta
9 Lucrecia
10 Mercado del Carmen
11 Mi Compa Chava
12 Pepe Coyotes
13 San Ángel Inn
14 Sud 777
15 La Taberna del León
16 Tacos Chupacabras
17 Tacos de Canasta Beto
18 Tetetlán
19 Tostadas Coyoacán
20 El Venadito

SHOPPING

1 El Bazaar Sábado
2 La Contra Coyoacán
3 Gallina de Guinea
4 Mercado de Coyoacán
5 Taller Experimental de Cerámica

COYOACÁN,
SAN ÁNGEL & ENVIRONS
DINING

One of the oldest parts of Mexico City, the delegación (borough) of Coyoacán is the entryway to what chilangos call "the south" of the metropolis. Its name derives from the native Náhuatl language, meaning "place of coyotes." While it wasn't until the 1850s that Coyoacán fully incorporated into the then Federal District, the area's history dates back to prehispanic times, founded by the Tepanec people to later become the base of Hernán Cortés's army during the conquest of Tenochtitlan, and the site of the earliest Spanish settlements in the Valley of Mexico.

Nowadays, Coyoacán's architecture reflects centuries-old Mexico City history with its central plazas, churches, colonial mansions, cobbled streets, and bohemian spirit. Among Coyoacán's most lustrous inhabitants were artists Frida Kahlo and her husband Diego Rivera, laureate poet Octavio Paz, and

Russian exile Leon Trotsky. Its one hundred colonias (neighborhoods) today combine traditional family-friendly communities with progressive art, culture, and counterculture. If you visit Casa Azul, Frida Kahlo's home-turned-museum, consider spending the day experiencing Coyoacán's central squares, markets, parks, and considerable charm.

San Ángel and Pedregal are upscale neighborhoods worth visiting in the city's south side, en route to southern boroughs like Tlalpan, Milpa Alta, and Xochimilco, home of the tourist-favorite floating gardens and colorful trajineras (canal boats), which are technically within the Mexico City limits but feel like separate towns and aren't reflected in this guide. San Ángel and Pedregal are connected by heavily trafficked avenues that cross a volcanic rock landscape filled with malls, shopping centers, and colonial to midcentury mansions hidden behind ivy and bougainvillea-covered walls. These neighborhoods boast maze-like residential streets, colorful markets, and museums to enjoy while soaking up the social and culinary life of the area.

1. Los Almendros
Avenida Insurgentes Sur 1759, colonia Guadalupe Inn

This restaurant started in a small Yucatecan town in 1962, expanding to Mexico City in 1990. It's still one of the best spots in the city for traditional Yucatecan cuisine in a white-tablecloth setting. Try it for breakfast, when you can get classic panuchos (fried bean-stuffed tortillas topped with pork or turkey), or eggs myriad ways, like "Xtooksel"—over a fat tortilla stuffed with white beans, pumpkin seeds, and herbs—or alongside longaniza de Valladolid, a smoked sausage from central Yucatán. Go with a group at lunch to try textbook versions of every classic dish from the gastronomically revered region.

2. La Barraca Valenciana
Centenario 91-C, colonia Del Carmen

La Barraca Valenciana has been the go-to place for Spanish-style tortas in Coyoacán for the past thirty-five years. Founded by José García, the small torta shop is now run by his son, chef José Miguel García, who has incorporated a selection of Mexican craft beers, Spanish sangria, and the red wine cocktail tinto de verano. Start with tapas like patatas bravas or ham croquettes, then order one of the unique torta offerings, such as Del Mar (squid with chimichurri), gallega (salt cod), or Blanc i Negre (butifarra and morcilla sausage).

3. Chamorros Coyoacán
Madrid 29, colonia Del Carmen

This is a family-run eatery serving one of the best chamorros (pork shanks), prepared carnitas-style (braised in its own fats and juices) in Mexico City. The shank comes to your table full-size and bone-in, and easily feeds two people with a pile of tortillas, salsas, onions, cilantro, and

5. Los Danzantes

Parque Centenario 12, colonia Villa Coyoacán

Los Danzantes has a special place in the history of Coyoacán's restaurant scene. Founded in 1995 as a branch of their original Oaxaca location, Los Danzantes was among the first restaurants to offer an upscale dining experience in the adjacent central plazas of Jardín Centenario and Jardín Hidalgo, which are now ringed by several attractive restaurants. It features modern interpretations of traditional Oaxacan dishes and a wide selection of mezcals from Oaxaca (including their own brands, Los Danzantes and Mezcal Alipús). Los Danzantes has become a destination for fans of both traditional and contemporary Oaxacan food and drink.

lime wedges (order beans separately—they're terrific). There's also an almost comically long menu of other traditional Mexican dishes, including many vegetarian options.

4. Corazón de Maguey

Parque Centenario 9A, colonia Villa Coyoacán

For more than a decade, Corazón de Maguey has showcased traditional Mexican food and agave spirits in a space that feels very Coyoacán: a dining room with bright red and blue walls, colorful prehispanic inspired murals, and outdoor seating overlooking Jardín Centenario and its iconic fountain of frisky coyotes. Expect casual dining and family-friendly vibes with Oaxacan favorites like tlayudas (large comal-crisped tortillas with toppings), jamaica (hibiscus) tacos, and a seven-mole tasting paired with handmade tortillas. The mezcal selection is long and the pours are generous.

6. Eloise Chic Cuisine

Avenida Revolución 1521, colonia San Ángel

Eloise elevated the dining scene in the San Ángel area when it first opened in 2011. The menu from chefs Abel Hernández and Nasheli Martínez is contemporary French punched up with local ingredients, like their iconic foie gras crème brûlée with passion fruit vinaigrette, a berry salad with local goat cheese and guava, and a fennel-mint soubise with a rack of lamb and barley "risotto" that hints at the flavors of green mole. Also recommended is their nearby sister restaurant, Loretta, which offers more of a pan-Mediterranean menu.

7. Guadiana
Pedro Luis Ogazón 102, colonia Guadalupe Inn
Guadiana is part of the Grupo Hunan restaurant group, which started with an upscale Chinese restaurant in the early 1990s and now counts more than two dozen concepts. It's an elegant choice for a long lunch, with an expansive menu that's equal parts taquería (crispy duck tacos, fish tacos al pastor), steakhouse (mesquite grilled bone-in tenderloin and an immaculate steak tartare), and seafood shack (pistachio and chile-crusted tuna, fish meatballs stuffed with huauzontle, aka Aztec broccoli).

8. La Jacinta
Plaza San Jacinto 3, colonia San Ángel
La Jacinta plays with the concept of the Mexican cantina, adding a contemporary twist. The menu includes terrific versions of homespun fare like cochinita tacos, mole enchiladas, and tortilla soup, while the cocktail selection is heavy on margaritas and mojitos. The ambiance is lively, casual, and family-friendly during the day, becoming more drinks-heavy as night falls.

9. Lucrecia
Simarruba 139b, colonia El Rosario
This is a friendly, unpretentious spot for unique moles (fig, beet, etc.) and vegetarian dishes like plantain-stuffed ancho chiles and hibiscus flautas (see page 119), but it's at its best for breakfast, before a visit to nearby Museo Anahuacalli. Try a huitlacoche (see page 56) omelet with red mole, or enfrijoladas (bean-sauce tortillas) with chorizo-scrambled eggs (see page 55).

10. Mercado del Carmen
Calle de la Amargura 5, colonia San Ángel
Not a "mercado" in the sense of the traditional neighborhood market, this is an upscale food court in a busy, attractive part of San Ángel. Mercado del Carmen offers more than thirty mostly food stands to indulge in pastries, coffee, gelato, chocolates, Mexican wine, craft beer, and heartier fare as well. It's located next to El Bazaar Sábado, the bustling indoor-outdoor

Saturday street fair, so go on a weekend to hit two birds with one stone. Mercado del Carmen also has live music during the weekends.

11. Mi Compa Chava
Calle Presidente Venustiano Carranza 109, colonia Villa Coyoacán
A project that started as a ghost kitchen during the pandemic has become one of the most sought-after restaurants for seafood in Mexico City; the Coyoacán outpost is a good way to (partially) avoid the endless waits at the Roma location (page 15). Both have the same menu, featuring fresh produce from Sinaloa and Baja California to create an array of Mexican seafood classics like zarandeado shrimp and fish, seafood cocktails and tostadas, a raw seafood bar, and aguachiles (see page 53).

12. Pepe Coyotes
Avenida Miguel Hidalgo 297, colonia Del Carmen
Pepe Coyotes has been delighting chilangos with oversized tacos since 1985. The original location of the taquería sits inside Mercado de Coyoacán and is a household name in Coyoacán thanks to its significant portions and variety of alambres, a jumble of grilled meats, bell peppers, onion, and bacon. Pepe Coyotes has

an alambre for every palate: beef, pork, chicken, shrimp, veggie, or a combination of all the above.

13. San Ángel Inn

Diego Rivera 50, colonia San Ángel

Within a few steps of the Diego Rivera and Frida Kahlo studio (not to be confused with Frida's Casa Azul), San Ángel Inn is a legendary Mexican hacienda-turned-restaurant admired for its colonial beauty, dedicated service, and upscale Mexican dishes like abalone with chipotle, fideo seco (thin noodles cooked in salsa) with foie gras, and a tableside Caesar salad (invented in Tijuana). The restaurant is a regular for politicians, socialites, and tourists drawn to the formal old-school atmosphere and the tranquil courtyard. To soak in the vibes without committing to a meal, ask to be seated on the periphery of the courtyard for terrific cocktails (martinis come with a sidecar) and maybe a duck taco—or six.

14. Sud 777

Boulevard de la Luz 777, colonia Jardines del Pedregal

One of the city's most acclaimed restaurants is tucked inside the prosperous Jardines de Pedregal neighborhood. Chef Edgar Núñez describes his work in Sud 777 as "vegetable

cuisine" because it emphasizes working with local producers and the restaurant's own gardens to grow what is on the plate. But while the tasting menu is largely vegan (and recommended), there's plenty of meat and seafood to order à la carte as well, like a kampachi tostada, Veracruz-style beef tongue, or trout with cauliflower pureé.

15. La Taberna del León

Antonio Plaza Altamirano 46, colonia Tizapán San Ángel

In the late 1970s, Mónica Patiño's first restaurant, La Taberna del León, pioneered upscale Mexican cuisine in its initial countryside location in Valle de Bravo. She went on to become one of the most influential Mexico City chefs and still innovates with her take on Mexican fine dining, sourcing local ingredients while blending international flavors and techniques with Mexican culinary traditions. The restaurant is perfect for a business lunch, dinner, or celebratory date.

16. Tacos Chupacabras

Río Churubusco and Avenida México (under highway), colonia Del Carmen

One of the quintessential late-night street taquerías of Coyoacán, Tacos Chupacabras—aka "Los Chupas"—has been around for more than twenty years, and the secret behind its most famous eponymous taco is, according to owner-taquero Guillermo Matías de Hilario, the house seasoning composed of 127 spices. Whatever the cause, the resulting taco is a joyful mix of meats and sausage complemented by beans, mashed potatoes, cactus salad, and various salsas.

17. Tacos de Canasta Beto
Berlín 184,
colonia Del Carmen

Tacos de canasta (see page 117) are ubiquitous in Mexico City and are constantly on the move, nested inside baskets riding precariously on (and sold from) the back of bicycles. In Coyoacán, Tacos de Canasta Beto is a staple in the neighborhood and has adopted an official corner close to the Frida Kahlo house. The chicharrón (pork rind) or potato tacos are usually Beto's best options, but all are made extra-special by his habanero salsa with pineapple and cucumber.

18. Tetetlán
Avenida de Las Fuentes 180-B,
colonia Jardines del Pedregal

Tetetlán sits inside Casa Pedregal, a 1940s-era private home designed by legendary Mexican architect Luis Barragán. Tetetlán is many things: a library, a boutique shop, a space to exhibit local artists, and a casual café, and many Barragán devotees make the pilgrimage just to explore the house and grounds. If doing so, why not have a meal in the lovely Tetetlán? For breakfast, try organic eggs in a giant hoja santa leaf, which tastes faintly of root beer, with queso Ocosingo from Chiapas; for lunch, maybe a tlayuda (large comal-crisped tortilla) with chile-marinated pork, longaniza sausage, Oaxacan cheese, beans, and mole sauce.

19. Tostadas Coyoacán
Mercado de Coyoacán,
Ignacio Allende 49,
colonia Del Carmen

For many years, tostadas have been a synonym for Coyoacán's food scene because of the colossal piles of twenty-plus toppings to be generously dolloped on large and crunchy corn tostadas. Though the market boasts several tostada stands, the "original" tostada mecca—dating back to the mid-1950s—is known as Tostadas Coyoacán, recognizable for its giant yellow and orange signs. Pin a visit to the market around eleven in the morning, since the tostada aisle can be hectic and crowded as lunch hour approaches, especially on Sundays.

20. El Venadito
Avenida Universidad 1701,
colonia Agrícola

With more than seventy years under its belt preparing Hidalgo-style carnitas, El Venadito is a family-run casual eatery with a short but sweet menu of carnitas and barbacoa tacos (see page 116). The restaurant has remained virtually unchanged for the past four decades, much to the delight of a passionate clientele that starts lining up before ten A.M. on weekends. (Once a weekends-only spot, it's now open daily until six P.M.) El Venadito is a timeless Coyoacán gem.

COYOACÁN, SAN ÁNGEL & ENVIRONS
SHOPPING

The best shopping areas of Coyoacán and San Ángel are where you're likely to be anyway: Jardín Centenario and Jardín Hidalgo in Coyoacán, and Plaza San Jacinto in San Ángel. Besides the places below, roam the charming streets around these central plazas to find small boutiques and spontaneous outdoor markets.

1. El Bazaar Sábado
Plaza San Jacinto 11, colonia San Ángel

There's arguably no better place to be on Saturdays than this weekly indoor-outdoor art and design market, centered on the pretty Plaza San Jacinto and stretching blocks in every direction. Among the hundred-plus vendors are modern ceramics, textiles, crafts, and artisanal food products, as well as vintage kitchenware and silver serving pieces. Be sure to check out the brick-and-mortar furniture shops that face the plaza, as well as the gorgeous Iglesia y Exconvento de San Jacinto, a church complex dating to the 1500s.

2. La Contra Coyoacán
Avenida Miguel Hidalgo 9-Local 10, colonia Del Carmen

With several locations in Mexico (and two in Mexico City), this all-Mexican wine shop has played an important role in educating locals about the variety and quality of Mexican wine. Buy a few bottles here for a hotel-room tasting, and strike up a conversation with the expert staff about the many burgeoning wine regions across the country.

3. Gallina de Guinea

General Aureliano Rivera 4, colonia Del Carmen

This chic cookbook shop is a must-visit for fans of the genre. There are books in English and Spanish, many of them unavailable in the United States.

4. Mercado de Coyoacán

Ignacio Allende No. 49, colonia San Ángel

Conveniently located in Coyoacán's most touristy section, this rambling market is one of the city's cheeriest. Many come for the famed tostada stands, but meat loversshould do like the locals and come on weekend mornings for

barbacoa (see page 116). There are also a lot of smaller vendors with kitchenware and crafts (skulls and skeletons seem to be especially popular here).

5. Taller Experimental de Cerámica

Centenario 63, colonia Del Carmen

Some of the city's best restaurants use dishes from this influential ceramics workshop, founded in the 1960s by Alberto Díaz de Cossio, and it's now open to the public every day except Sunday. It's a must-visit for beautiful but practical dishware and unique serving pieces that will survive the flight back. The hefty, high-fired ceramics (which makes them much harder and stronger than the low-fired ceramics more common in traditional markets)

have unusual, inventive glazes that are both vividly modern and a nod to the country's rich ceramics history. They also have a booth at El Bazaar Sábado (opposite) in San Ángel.

BEYOND RESTAURANTS

Coffee Shops
Café Avellaneda
Café El Jarocho
Café Lance
Café Negro
Marabunta

Bars
La Bipo
Doble Malta
Júpiter Cervecería
Mezcalero Coyoacán

Bakeries
Bakers
El Olvidado
Pancracia
Ruta de la Seda

Sweets
Beyond Sugar
Ki' Xocolatl
El Portal de Sabor
Tout Chocolat

TACOS

By Bill Esparza

Just to be clear from the start: If it's in a tortilla, it's a taco. Rolled or folded, corn or flour, and any filling imaginable—it all counts. The taco is the means and the end, the medium and the message. Grilled fish served with tortillas? That's fish tacos. A burrito is just a big taco de harina (flour tortilla taco), usually crisped on a grill or comal. There are tacos de sal—nothing more than salt sprinkled on a freshly made tortilla—and even tacos de nada (nothing tacos), which are, as the name might imply, just folded or rolled tortillas, albeit usually topped with salsa, cheese, and maybe onions, cilantro, and lettuce or cabbage. No matter the style, tacos are not complete until you garnish to taste with salsa and, ideally, a squeeze of lime.

While the taco is perhaps the number-one icon of the Mexican culinary canon, it's a relatively recent term, if not invention. Indigenous Mexicans have been eating tortillas with other foods for centuries, but there are only two mentions of tacos in Mexican literature prior to 1891: in an 1836 cookbook telling readers to roll a stuffed pork loin "like a taco de tortilla," and an 1861 novel whose character eats a "taco de tortilla" spread with chiles. But it was Manuel Payno's hugely popular 1891 novel *Los Bandidos de Río Frío*, and its scene of a goat taco celebration, that brought the term to common parlance. It was included four years later in the definitive *Diccionario de mejicanismos*, a dictionary of Mexican words that were unknown, or used differently, in Castilian Spanish.

Fast-forward to today, when Mexico City offers an endless feast of tacos, 24/7, served from puestos (see page 56), brick-and-mortar taquerías (see , bicycles, and any setup that industrious taqueros can concoct to feed more than twenty-one million locals in the metropolitan area. The city's sheer size, and the fact that CDMX is home to people from all over the country (every region has its own taco traditions), makes it Mexico's most prolific and varied taco culture.

In busy areas, barely a block goes by without seeing people from all walks of life huddled around open-air stands, and it's not uncommon to find one city block containing more than a dozen different taco establishments. The economic incentive of feeding the armies of workers looking for a fast meal on the go attracts cutthroat competition, creating a vast landscape of inexpensive, well-constructed, high-quality tacos emerging from plumes of steam into eager hands.

While tacos have certainly infiltrated fine dining, taco culture in Mexico City remains the stuff of street food. And unlike most of the city's rigidly timed culinary traditions, tacos are eaten at any time of day: Morning tacos de canasta (see page 117) are as much a part of the city's fabric as after-hours tacos de suadero (see page 57). As a visitor, don't stress about knowing all the rules and customs around tacos. Each taco, taquero, and taquería is different, and every taco you try will give you a little more confidence and knowledge to tackle the city's best.

These eleven styles of tacos remain the backbone of Mexico's capital, where corn tortillas reign supreme and a taco tour is a clever strategy for visitors to absorb some of the best parts of Mexico City cuisine, one taco at a time.

TACOS AL CARBÓN

It wasn't too long ago that, if locals wanted traditional northern-style carne asada—flame-grilled beef—they had to make do with one of the many terrific Argentinian steakhouses in town. Now, however, with food from the Mexican north more popular than ever, it's possible to experience legit carne asada all over the city. Tacos al carbón refers to tacos of any thin-cut meat cooked over wood or charcoal fire (as opposed to a griddle, as with tacos de plancha), but the best are usually found at places that model themselves after the premier spots in northern Mexico.

At **Los de Asada** in the businesslike Nápoles neighborhood, diners can order whole porterhouse, cowboy (bone-in rib eye), and Kansas City strip steaks, or choose from more than a dozen tacos filled with picanha (sirloin cap), cecina (partially dried beef with or without a chile rub), pork belly, and bone marrow, among others. At the center of the action is a large circular barbecue pit made of bricks. On the side, order carne en su jugo, beef broth with onion, cilantro, and radish.

Los de Asada
Kansas 93, colonia Nápoles

TACOS DE BARBACOA

Barbacoa is traditional pit-roasted meat wrapped in maguey (agave) leaves. Typically, you'll find it done with lamb or goat in southern and central Mexico, while beef rules in the north. Barbacoa is often served with a consomé broth made from the meat drippings and juices, as well as offal dishes like pancita (stomach), montalayo (offal-stuffed stomach), and moronga (blood sausage). Tacos de barbacoa are typically eaten with salsas and other condiments that vary by region. Across CDMX, most barbacoa stands represent styles from different parts of the nearby states of Hidalgo and México.

Barbacoa is a weekend treat from rural families who bring it from outside the city, and it's not difficult to find barbacoa stands across CDMX on Saturday and Sunday mornings. **Barbacoa Los 3 Reyes** has an on-site pit for a true taste of Estado de México in the Mixcoac neighborhood a few miles south of Chapultepec Park. The recipe was created by Álvaro González from El Oro, Estado de México, who learned it from his father. Show up early (they open at eight thirty A.M. and start running out of some cuts by one) for moist lamb barbacoa and to make your own tacos with fresh-made blue corn tortillas, salsa borracha (chile pasilla with pulque), and pápalo (a wild herb) accompanied by cold beers and micheladas for your breakfast drinking.

Barbacoa Los 3 Reyes
Pablo Veronés 12, colonia Alfonso XIII

TACOS DE CANASTA

The regional name for steamed tacos—"canasta" meaning "basket"—is due to the tradition of transporting stacked tacos in large baskets, often on bicycles, wrapped in a towel to keep them warm and supple. These days, the quaint baskets are just as often insulated beverage coolers or steel pots. They're also called tacos sudados—sweated tacos—to reiterate the moistness that these enclosures ensure. Common fillings in CDMX are chicharrón (pork rinds) in green salsa, mole verde, adobo, refried beans and potatoes, with salsas and pickled chiles with vegetables as complements. These small steamed tacos filled with tasty stews inside of thin, oily corn tortillas are a popular breakfast and lunchtime snack.

Since 1971, **Tacos Joven** in the great taco neighborhood of Narvarte has drawn daytime crowds for its quality ingredients and larger-than-usual tacos de canasta. Standouts are the mole verde, chicharrón (pork rinds), and deshebrada (shredded beef) fillings, topped with either chunky avocado salsa or salsa morichi (chile morita with plump stewed chicharrón), and a side of pickled jalapeños.

Tacos Joven
Avenida Universidad 199-B, colonia Vértiz Narvarte

TACOS DE CABEZA

Eyes, cheeks, lips, tongue, brains—these are some of the delicacies that fall under the tacos de cabeza category, more popular in CDMX than most visitors might expect. Most fritanga joints will have tacos de cabeza as well, but it's worth checking out a specifically cabeza taquería if you can find one.

Hop in the line at **Tacos El Paisa** with an appetite right when they open at five thirty P.M., because these tacos go fast. An order comes with enough fatty meat to make a half-dozen tacos with yellow corn tortillas that are steamed along with the meat before serving. Cachete (cheek) is always a favorite, as are ojos (eyes) for a more gelatinous cut. Can't decide? Surtida is a mix of cuts finished with red onions minced with habanero and jalapeño, good with both red and green salsas and lots of lime wedges to balance the meat's unctuous richness.

Tacos El Paisa
Tehuantepec 56B, colonia Roma Sur

TACOS DE CARNITAS

Nose-to-tail pork cuts fried in their own fat, confit-style, are known by the modest moniker of "carnitas." They're a specialty of the state of Michoacán, though they're common throughout central and western Mexico and beyond. Some popular cuts include panza (tripe), chamorro (shank), costilla (rib), nana (uterus), buche (pork stomach), and offal in general. Maciza refers to lean meat without skin or gristle (usually from the loin and shoulder), surtida is a little bit of everything, and achica-lada is usually an off-menu offering that is essentially the dregs of the fry vat—think burnt ends.

In 1978 Roberto Sapien moved from Zacapu, Michoacán, where he learned to cook carnitas, to Mexico's capital to open **Rincón Tarasco**, one of the city's carnitas institutions. Sapien's carnitas are deeply flavored with browned, crispy edges, and brightened with his vinegary salsa made of chile manzano (like a bigger, less spicy habanero). The Pedro Chávez combo (buche with belly skin) and despanzada, a special pork belly cut exclusive to this restaurant, are two of the proprietary tacos that set this taquería apart.

Rincón Tarasco
Comercio 131, colonia Escandón

TACOS DORADOS/ FLAUTAS

Tacos dorados and flautas are the same thing—rolled tacos fried in oil or lard—but for their size: Flautas (aka flutes) are longer. They're filled with simple things like shredded chicken, potato, or cheese, and dressed with crema, crumbled cheese, shredded lettuce or cabbage, and salsa. They're sometimes served ahogadas, which translates to "drowned," but in practice the flautas are just partially immersed in a shallow bowl of sauce.

There's a constant line for Doña Magos's extra-long flautas at her namesake flautería, **Flautas Magos**, in colonia Peralvillo, which has been in the family for seventy years. It's obligatory to order three flautas at a minimum, which she garnishes with a copious amount of Mexican crema, a scattering of chopped white onion, and a ladleful of salsa (tip: order salsa campechana, which includes both salsas: spicy chile morita and

a salsa verde of chile serrano with tomatillos). Drag the flautas across the Styrofoam plate to gather up a little of everything before taking a bite.

Flautas Magos
Adelina Patti 119, colonia Peralvillo

TACOS DE FRITANGA

Tacos de fritanga are made from various cuts of meat, such as longaniza (see page 55), tripas (see page 57), suadero (see page 57), and always some offal cuts, seasoned and fried with lard in a charola, a shallow stainless-steel disc with a raised convex dome in the middle.

Open 24/7 in the Centro Histórico, **Taquería Los Cocuyos** is the destination for most taco tours in CDMX for tacos de fritanga, and the benchmark for the style. The first order must be suadero, then campechano (tongue and longaniza), then maybe cachete (beef cheek), ojos (eyes), or trompa (snout) piled on supple white-corn tortillas with onion and cilantro. Finish with a smoky brick-red salsa, avocado salsa, or tart salsa verde, and a squeeze of lime before digging into one of CDMX's street food icons.

Taquería Los Cocuyos
Simón Bolívar 59, colonia Centro

TACOS DE GUISADO

Tacos de guisado are corn tortillas filled with an infinite variety of pre-made stews, braises, and whatever else the taqueros feel fit to prepare, and usually topped with a layer of Mexican rice to absorb the juices. With hundreds, if not thousands, of recipes served at tacos de guisado stands, visitors to the city will barely make a dent, but at **Los Cazuelas de Don José**, located inside a garage in delegación Tláhuac (in the southeast corner of the city), around twenty different stews will satisfy diners of all stripes. Look for fillings like tortitas de carne (meat and potato patties), costillas con nopales (pork rib and cactus in a morita chile sauce), and huevos al albañil (literally "bricklayer's eggs," eggs scrambled in a mild salsa).

Los Cazuelas de Don José
Olivos 87, colonia Los Olivos

TACOS DE HÍGADO

Though uncommon in the rest of the city, liver and onion tacos rule the streets of Tepito, a historic and notoriously rough-and-tumble neighborhood within colonia Morelos. Since 1973, Martín Ramírez Ruiz has been grilling liver and onions on his long plancha at the corner of Matamoros and Toltecas at his beloved neighborhood stand, **Tacos de Hígado Ramírez Moranchel**. He serves them with raw onion, cilantro, and your choice of bright red salsa.

Tacos de Hígado Ramírez Moranchel
Matamoros 163, colonia Morelos

TACOS AL PASTOR/ TACOS ÁRABES

Tacos al pastor are among CDMX's most emblematic tacos, where slabs of chile- and achiote-marinated pork shoulder and loin are piled on a trompo (vertical spit) and roasted by the hissing, spitting flames. The meat is sawed off in thin slivers and placed in small tortillas with onion, cilantro, and, often, grilled pineapple. Tacos árabes feature a related trompo style of meat, usually marinated without chiles, and served on pan árabe, thick flour tortillas that resemble pita.

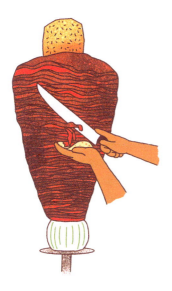

TACOS A LA PLANCHA

Tacos a la plancha are meats cooked on a flat top, and are among the most common tacos found on the streets of CDMX. Here is where diners can order tacos campechanos (combinations), the most popular being longaniza (sausage), bistec (thin-cut beef), or cecina (partially dried beef), and crumbled chicharrón (pork rinds). Other cuts include chuleta (pork chop), costilla (boneless pork rib), pechuga (chicken breast), and quesocarne (meat with melted cheese). "Alambre" refers to a mix of meats with onions and peppers, and often includes bacon and melted cheese as well, fried into a kind of a hash.

For campechanos, Don Rafael and Doña Elizabeth's **El Villamelón**, located next to the monumental Plaza de Toros as a gathering place for bullfight fans, has been the place to go since 1961. Their version is a textbook mix of chicharrón, longaniza, and cecina.

El Villamelón
Eje 6 Sur Tintoreto 123,
colonia Ciudad de los Deportes

In CDMX, myriad al pastor vendors can be found in every section of the city—even at trendy taquerías with Mexican craft beer and valet parking. **El Huequito** opened its first branch in 1959 and now has ten locations, which are conveniently located and remain among the city's best. Order more tacos than you think you'll want (they're small), and anoint them with the orange chile salsa or a creamy salsa verde with avocado, or get the Pastor Especial, an almost half-pound mini-mountain of meat with both salsas and a pile of tortillas basted with trompo drippings, for you to assemble your own taco feast.

El Huequito
Multiple locations, elhuequito.mx

COMIDA CORRIDA

Imagine, if you will, that dinner fell smack in the middle of the workday. Now imagine that you live in a sprawling metropolis where commutes can approach two hours each way. Such is the case in Mexico City, where la comida—usually translated as "lunch" but more accurately means "the meal"—generally starts between two and four P.M., when most workers are unable to go home to eat. The dilemma has resulted in a dining culture that reaches its vibrant peak in the midafternoon.

Most Mexico City guides might lead you to think that the city's food options fall into two categories: leisurely sit-down restaurants and street food. Yet in between the two are fondas (see page 56), smaller and usually family-owned restaurants that specialize in comida corrida, a frequently changing set-price menu offered only in the afternoon.

Comida corrida has no rules per se, but usually centers around a choice of homestyle main dishes—some version of meat in sauce, plus maybe milanesa (cutlet), chiles rellenos, and tacos or enchiladas—with a brothy soup and either rice or pasta to start, and a simple dessert to finish. Service can be hasty, as comida corrida is more of a workhorse meal than a social outing, but no one will mind if you linger. An agua fresca del día (fresh fruit water of the day) is usually offered gratis, with other drinks available for separate purchase.

For budget travelers, a good comida corrida can be a godsend, a satisfying traditional meal among locals for half the price of what one cocktail will cost you at hot restaurants and bars. The best way to find a favorite is to scour your neighborhood for the trademark dry-erase boards or chalkboard signs and look for a full house. Otherwise, here are ten to check out:

Cocina Angelita
Calle Camino a Nextengo 130-2, colonia Santa Cruz Acayucan
At the end of an alley next to a colorful cemetery and a cool modernist church is Cocina Angelita, popular among neighborhood workers at both breakfast and lunch with its wide selection and attention to detail.

La Delicia del Buen Comer
José Martí 39, colonia Tacubaya
Stop here before or after visiting the gorgeous Museo Casa de la Bola. The friendly service doesn't stop even when it's crowded with hungry locals and roaming guitarists. The albondigas (meatballs) have a loyal following.

La Esquina del Sabor
Calzada Santa Cruz 168, colonia Portales Norte
The menu at this attractive corner fonda can range from fresh grilled fish and chicken cordon bleu to more rustic dishes like vertiginous tostadas of pata (cow's foot) or tinga de pollo (shredded chicken in a chile sauce).

Las Flores

San Camilito a2, Centro Histórico

This is a non-touristy option when visiting the mariachi haven of Plaza Garibaldi. Choose from hearty, meaty mains like pork chops in a spicy cream sauce, chicharrón (pork rinds) in salsa verde, or liver and onions.

Fonda La Reforma

Calle Heroes and Degollado, colonia Guerrero

Located just off the massive Mercado Martínez de la Torre in colonia Guerrero, this fonda has been around since the late 1920s, and seemingly little has changed. Try the textbook chiles rellenos.

Fonda Roma

Cedro 113-1C, colonia Santa María la Ribera

The mains here are more ambitious than at most comida corrida spots, like the fish in a sauce of earthy pasilla chile and guava. The kitchen is equally generous with vegetables, like chard, chayote, and nopales (cactus paddles).

Fonda Siete

Ejido de San Francisco Culhuacán 199, colonia Presidentes Ejidales

This tiny gem is in a much less-touristed part of Coyoacán, worth visiting to see just how far Coyoacán stretches. Here, uncommon to many comida corrida joints, there are vegetarian as well as à la carte options.

La Güera

Merida 215, colonia Roma Norte

With all the culinary pretense in colonia Roma, La Güera's soulful home cooking and friendly familial atmosphere really hit the spot. A delicious pozole is offered most Fridays and Saturdays.

Martina Fonda Fina

Calle General Juan Cano 61, colonia San Miguel Chapultepec

The San Miguel Chapultepec neighborhood is popular among creative types who like its central park-adjacent location and discreet residential vibe. This stylish fonda fits right in, with beautifully executed dishes in a casually stylish and sunny room.

Receta Mínima

Calle Doctor Velasco 133, colonia Doctores

There are often interesting vegetarian options at this friendly hideaway a few blocks east of colonia Roma, like broccoli fritters in a gently spicy tomato broth, as well as meatier mains like pigs' feet or a veal cutlet.

Ciudad de los
Deportes
Del Valle Centro
Del Valle Norte
Del Valle Sur
Jamaica
Narvarte Oriente
Narvarte Poniente

Portales Norte
Portales Sur
San Simón
Tlacoquemecatl
del Valle
Vertiz Narvarte
Viaducto Piedad

DEL
NARV

6

VALLE &
ARTE

JAMAICA ②

ALEMÁN VALDÉS

VIADUCTO PIEDAD

⑩

CALZ. DE TLALPAN

AV. PDTE. PLUTARCO ELÍAS CALLES

RTE
TE

N

S

DEL VALLE & NARVARTE

DINING

① Alay Alay
② Balkan Grill
③ Barbacoa el Tulancingo
④ El Convite Fonda y Café
⑤ Don Calín
⑥ Dong Zi Gongfu Te
⑦ Fonda Margarita
⑧ Los Forcados
⑨ Huaraches Los Portales
⑩ Ka Won Seng
⑪ Lar Gallego
⑫ Mixtli
⑬ Norteñito Steak
⑭ Pez Muy Muy
⑮ Los Picudos
⑯ Las Polas
⑰ Los Pumpos
⑱ Restaurante Humbertos
⑲ El Rey de las Ahogadas
⑳ Romulo's
㉑ Salón Los Cuates
㉒ La Secina
㉓ Los Sopes de La Nueve
㉔ Suntory
㉕ Tacos "Beto"
   Los de Cochinada
㉖ Tacos Manolo
㉗ Tierra Adentro Cocina
㉘ El Villamelón
㉙ El Vilsito

SHOPPING

① Biblos
② Mercado de Jamaica
③ Mercado Del Valle
④ Mercado Lázaro Cárdenas
   Del Valle (for Café Passmar)
⑤ Mercado Portales
⑥ Yamamoto

DEL VALLE & NARVARTE
DINING

The southern border of colonia Roma hits a hard stop at Viaducto Presidente Miguel Alemán Valdés, a major freeway that runs east to west through much of the city. Though it's not on most tourists' radar, the area between Roma and Coyoacán has a lot of appeal. Most of it falls in the delegación (borough) of Benito Juárez, which is small in area but supports fifty-six distinct colonias, among them Del Valle, Narvarte, Nápoles, and Portales. They boast a dense concentration of eating, drinking, shopping, and business, but with attractive side streets and residential buildings that make it a popular place to live and work.

Colonia Nápoles is dominated by the World Trade Center complex, which includes a fifty-story office building, hotels, shopping centers, and the Polyforum Cultural Siquieros. The latter is a cultural exhibition center best known for its massive indoor-outdoor mural by David Alfaro Siquieros, *The March of Humanity*, which measures almost one hundred thousand square feet in total. At the other end of the borough is Portales, with the busy Mercado de Portales and the family-friendly Parque de los Venados. Narvarte is known for being a haven for taco lovers thanks to the quantity, quality, and variety of its taquerías. This whole "near south" area is verdant as well, with more than a dozen parks measuring several square blocks each. It's a terrific part of town to spend the day in.

1. Alay Alay

Matías Romero 98-Local 2, colonia Del Valle Centro

This colorful taquería shows how naturally—and deliciously—Mexican and Middle Eastern food can coexist beyond tacos árabes (see page 120). Served on your choice of fresh-made pita or corn tortillas, there are tacos and costras (cheese-crusted tacos) of fried chicken and muhammara, Yemeni-spiced pork, and turkey with dates and tahini. Order all the traditional spreads to slather on like salsas. To drink, choose from Mexican wines, craft beer, and an interesting list of nonalcoholic drinks, like a strawberry limeade with cardamom and orange flower water.

2. Balkan Grill

Xola 1615, colonia Narvarte Poniente

This Serbian resturant is known for its wide range of cheese-stuffed pljeskavica (Serbian burgers), with three dressings: ajvar (roasted red pepper), tarator (Greek yogurt and cucumber), and urnebes (a spicy cheese spread). Come with a group, though, to try other Serbian dishes like ćevapi (fresh sausage), uštipci (savory fried dough), gibanica (a cheesy filo pie), and an appetizer platter of traditional cured meats and cheeses. To drink? Rakija (fruit brandy) or špricer (wine spritzer).

3. Barbacoa el Tulancingo

Calzada Santa Cruz 72, colonia Portales Norte

Barbacoa (see page 116) is a weekend tradition in Mexico City, the best of which is brought from nearby Hidalgo state where sheep are slow-roasted in earthen pits and the fall-off-the-bone meat is served with fresh tortillas, onions, nopales (cactus paddles), chicharrón (pork rinds), fresh panela cheese, herbs, and multiple salsas. Grab a couple stools at one of the orange oilcloth-covered tables here to experience true Hidalgo-style barbacoa, open Saturdays and Sundays only from eight A.M. until they run out, usually late afternoon. Order by the kilo, on or off the bone, with bowls of

consomé (broth) and, if you're into it, panza (tripe) tacos or sesos (brains) quesadillas (see page 56), which you'll find on most tables even in the morning.

4. El Convite Fonda y Café
Ajusco 79 Bis,
colonia Portales Sur
As much an event space as a restaurant, El Convite hosts jazz concerts, art exhibitions, film screenings, and literary readings, and is involved with the curation and sponsorship of cultural events around the city. Its Italian-meets-steakhouse concept feels very Buenos Aires, as does the European bistro atmosphere and diverse clientele. The adjacent café is a great place for an afternoon coffee and pineapple tart.

5. Don Calín
Alhambra 210,
colonia Portales Norte
This cozy Yucatecan café (the owners are from the town of Valladolid in central Yucatán) is a popular lunch spot among local workers, but try it for a hearty breakfast before exploring the Portales market. Chilaquiles come topped with cochinita pibil, and there are eggs scrambled with chaya, a Yucatecan green hard to find in the city.

6. Dong Zi Gongfu Te
Dr. José María Vértiz 692,
colonia Narvarte Poniente
Though it sometimes seems possible, one cannot live on tacos alone. On a lazy weekend Mexico City morning, legit dim sum can be just the ticket. Dong Zi

Gongfu Te roughly translates to "winter solstice tea ceremony," but the appeal of this restaurant is its Hong Kong–style dim sum selection on Saturdays and Sundays from nine A.M. to two P.M. There is also a traditional a la carte menu on weekend evenings and the rest of the week, but bring cash, as they don't accept credit cards.

7. Fonda Margarita
Adolfo Prieto 1364 B,
colonia Tlacoquemecatl del Valle
This has been on many travelers' CDMX radar ever since Anthony Bourdain deemed it the best breakfast he'd ever had in 2009. Still, this tiny fonda had no problem filling seats before that, its bubbling cazuelas (clay pots) having served regulars since 1948.

The refried beans with egg and/or longaniza—rolled like a French omelet—are a must; otherwise just pick from traditional guisados (stewed dishes) like chicharrón (pork rinds) en salsa verde, bistec en salsa pasilla (steak in inky pasilla chile sauce), and tortas de cerdo (sandwiches with pork patties in tomato sauce). Come early, as many dishes are sold out by ten A.M.

8. Los Forcados
Alhambra 509,
colonia Portales Norte

Whether this place invented tacos campechanos (see page 53) is up for debate, but it likely has the city's best. Their "El Auténtico Campechano" features bistec, longaniza, and chicharrón (pork rinds) for a blast of textures and flavors, especially when paired with the exceptional salsas. The "Taco Forcadito" is a crispy cylinder of grilled Manchego cheese with chicken and mushrooms, and the "Taco Gaonita"— beef filet—is filled with meat softer than the tortilla. With a cheerful atmosphere and great service, this will become one of your favorite taquerías.

9. Huaraches Los Portales
Avenida Víctor Hugo 74,
colonia Portales Norte

Huaraches (see page 42), while delicious, can be a bit one-note when they're a thick, plate-sized tortilla barely sprinkled with toppings. Here, the huaraches themselves are long and narrow, light and tender, and generously garnished to keep the crucial balance between the huarache itself and the tasty toppings (twenty-two in total to choose from, including all kinds of meat, plus mushrooms, cheese, and egg). As the crew here is made up of master masa manipulators, the bargain-priced gorditas (see page 42) are fantastic as well.

10. Ka Won Seng
Albino García 362
Colonia Viaducto Piedad

Mexico City has two Chinatowns: a colorful but largely touristy one in the Centro Histórico, and a more interesting one, culinarily speaking, in colonia Viaducto Piedad, just east of Narvarte, where there is a concentration of Chinese immigrants. The extensive menu at Ka Won Seng can be daunting, especially since some items aren't translated from the Chinese characters, but it pays to explore with dishes like goose with sour plum, goat with tofu skin, and a mixed-vegetable dish with snow pea, lotus root, and spongy luffa (aka Chinese okra).

11. Lar Gallego
Insurgentes Sur 628
Colonia Del Valle Norte

In its fourth decade, this grand Galician restaurant (think mahogany walls, marble floors, and starched tablecloths) serves impeccable dishes from Galicia and elsewhere in northern Spain. Try garlicky angulas (baby eels) a la Bilbaína, grilled quail, and Solomillo Lar, beef tenderloin in a red wine–mushroom sauce with Galician peppers.

12. Mixtli
Parroquia 727,
colonia Del Valle Sur

Mixtli focuses on Mexican food with Oaxacan influences (or, perhaps, Oaxacan food with pan-Mexican influences) that doesn't water down the state's powerful flavors and distinctive ingredients. Try the pork jowl memela (see page 42) with lime, soy, spring onion, and a charred tomatillo salsa; duck in black mole with Brussels sprouts and chilacayote squash; and guacamole with assorted insects. It's also a great breakfast option. Our pick? Eggs in hoja santa (Mexican herb) with a flat white.

13. Norteñito Steak
La Morena 1210,
colonia Narvarte Oriente

Glitzy signage makes this place look like a fast-food outlet, but it's one of the best places for northern-

style carne asada. Tacos come on freshly made flour tortillas with rib eye, sirloin, or skirt steak; bacon-wrapped burritos are crisped on the grill; and don't miss the empalmes, a lard-fried tortilla sandwich from the state of Nuevo León with chicharrón (pork rinds), porky beans, shredded beef, or shaved pork.

14. Pez Muy Muy
Caleta 466,
colonia Narvarte Oriente

"Muy muy" (very very) is a great way to describe this colorful place that offers a broad survey of dishes from Mexico's northern Pacific coast. Burritos—not a common sight in Mexico City—are stuffed with shrimp, marlin, or chiles rellenos; there's a tlacoyo (see page 43) platter with toppings of roasted marlin, garlic octopus, and extra-spicy shrimp; tuna "carnitas" are crispy fish bites; and there are even seafood

chilaquiles. Start with the creamy shrimp soup, and to drink, choose from several clamato preparations, ideally with beer added.

15. Los Picudos
Moras 230,
colonia Tlacoquemecatl del Valle

Of all the taco types in the city, tacos al carbón (see page 116) might be the most beloved, even as they're not always easy to come by: Most tacos al carbón vendors use gas or electric grills instead of actual charcoal. Not the case at Los Picudos, where they have been plying tacos over red-hot coals since the eighties. The unadorned cuts of beef (bistec, arrachera) and pork (chuleta, costilla) are served with two salsas, a thin guacamole and a red sauce smoky with morita chile. Quesadillas are either corn tortillas or pan árabe (like thin pita bread), "flameadas" over the grill for exceptional flavor.

16. Las Polas
Avenida Colonia del Valle 505, colonia Del Valle Centro

It's Yucatecan with a twist at Las Polas, a sunny café off a busy six-way intersection in the heart of Del Valle. Try chiles güeros stuffed with minced pork and covered in two salsas, panuchos (fried bean-stuffed tortillas) topped with sour orange-marinated fish and smoky crumbled longaniza de Valladolid (a regional Yucatecan delicacy), and tender achiote-flecked tamales.

17. Los Pumpos
Alhambra 214,
colonia Portales Norte

The cuisine of the southern state of Chiapas gets little respect within the greater Mexican culinary canon—or at least little representation outside its borders—despite having much in common with its neighbor Oaxaca, whose cuisine is world-renowned. Chiapas is a haven for tamales, and Los Pumpos usually has at least eight different types, like one filled with chicken in a Chiapanecan mole made with raisins, olives, and almonds. For breakfast, try scrambled eggs and chorizo (see page 55) with beans and fried plantains.

18. Resaurante Humbertos

Patricio Sanz 1440,
colonia Tlacoquemecatl del Valle

Besides Yucatecan classics like cochinita pibil, relleno negro, papadzules, and poc chuc, this thirty-plus-year-old favorite also serves less-seen dishes like pigs feet pibil, shark and beans, and mucbipollo, a giant tamal. It doesn't stop at the Yucatán, though, as there are non-region-specific dishes like bone marrow tacos, salt cod tortas, and queso fundido with the corn fungus huitlacoche. It's a fun lunch for a group.

19. El Rey de las Ahogadas

Avenida Coyoacán 360-E,
colonia Del Valle Norte

Since it opened in 1963, the signature dish here has been flautas ahogadas, drenched in a warm, spicy salsa verde and topped with cotija cheese, onion, and cream. Don't stop there, though—the sopes (see page 42), huaraches (see page 42), quesadillas (see page 42), and gorditas (see page 42) are also great. Vegetarians should note that the various fillings include squash blossoms, cheese, huitlacoche (see page 56), potato, bean, spinach, mushroom, and roasted poblano chiles.

20. Romulo's

Mercado 1o de Diciembre, Yácatas 80 Locales 23-28
colonia Narvarte Poniente

Come lunchtime, there are more people at this long-standing market restaurant than there are people in the rest of the market combined. Start with oysters, clams, and pata de mula (blood clams) on the half shell and one of the city's best aguachiles (see page 53), then move on to shrimp or fish, prepared more than a dozen ways, or a seafood mixed grill to share. There's also a more recent location a half block north at Uxmal 52.

21. Salón Los Cuates

Calle Dr. José María Vértiz 823,
colonia Narvarte Poniente

Known for having the largest botana (see page 53) selection in town, this cantina has one hundred (yes, one hundred) dishes, separated into three courses (don't miss the garlic octopus), and all free with a minimum four-drink purchase

per person. It's easy to while away the hours here, especially after five P.M. when the live music starts, but less heavy drinkers or those in a hurry can order individual dishes à la carte. It's one of the few cantinas with outdoor seats, but you'll still want to sit inside to be part of the action.

22. La Secina

Casa del Obrero Mundial 305,
colonia Narvarte Poniente

Bright lights and colorful tile beckon you into this sprawling, cheery snack bar–meets–beer hall. The food comes from several Mexican states: Oaxacan tlayudas (large comal-crisped tortillas with layers of toppings), Yucatecan panuchos (fried, bean-stuffed tortillas), cecina from Morelos, carne seca from Chihuahua, and carne asada from Nuevo León. To drink, sample from several Mexican craft beers, the house pear-cilantro margarita, and bargain-priced mezcals.

23. Los Sopes de La Nueve
Luis Spota 85,
colonia San Simón

Though these jumbo oval sopes (see page 42) read more like huaraches (see page 42), they're undoubtedly among the archetypal sopes in the city. There are twenty-four toppings (including lamb, shrimp, bacon, and smoked pork chop), and combinations with several toppings piled atop each other. The carb-averse can even opt for a base of nopales instead of the usual corn tortilla masa. On weekends, there's pozole, paella, pancita (tripe), carnitas, and barbacoa (see page 116) in addition to the already-exhaustive menu of antojitos (page 53).

24. Suntory
Torres Adalid 14,
colonia Del Valle Norte

This restaurant opened in 1970 as the Japanese distilling conglomerate's first international restaurant and has since expanded to include several locations throughout the country. Its success helped spur a proliferation of high-end Japanese restaurants over the subsequent decades. Choose from teppanyaki (splurge on the imported A5 Wagyu), sushi and sashimi, and any number of other traditional dishes, but don't miss the butter clams and rib-eye tacos.

25. Tacos "Beto" Los de Cochinada
Calle Dr. José María Vértiz 1028,
colonia Vértiz Narvarte

It's often the most outlandish inventions that end up the most beloved. Tacos de cochinada were invented here by Don Beto in the mid-1960s, when, instead of discarding the burnt bits and pooled meat fats left over from frying suadero (see page 57) and longaniza, he added scoops of it to his tacos to add texture and flavor. Now, people line up for tacos "con cochi" and other taquerías have adopted the practice. Delightfully greasy and rich, they're a must for those with steel stomachs.

26. Tacos Manolo
Luz Saviñon 1305,
colonia Narvarte Poniente

The order here are the tacos "Manolo," a mix of steak, bacon, and onion on corn tortillas, for you to top with their signature salsa of chile de árbol and peanuts (on pan árabe, they call it a "juanga"). Groups of three or more should also consider the parrillada, with five kinds of meat, assorted vegetables, and melted cheese, served with stacks of tortillas. With large portions, varied salsas, and a constant stream of customers, it's a good place to start a taco tour of Narvarte.

27. Tierra Adentro Cocina
Avenida Nevado 112,
colonia Portales Sur

The beauty of Tierra Adentro is that it simultaneously adheres to tradition while constantly surprising with lesser-known regional dishes and smart tweaks on classics. Here you might find segueza (Oaxaca), aporreadillo (Michoacán), and tatemado colimote (Colima), plus specialties like huitlacoche on the cob, mushrooms in pistachio mole, and a guava tamal for dessert. The unpretentious, eclectic approach is a nice antidote to flashy Roma and Condesa hotspots.

28. El Villamelón
Eje 6 Sur Tintoreto 123,
colonia Ciudad de los Deportes

El Villamelón opened in 1961 across from Mexico City's Plaza de Toros, the world's largest bullfighting ring, and remains one of the city's most iconic Mexico City taquerías. The owners squabble with Los Forcados over who invented tacos campechanos (see page 53), but as long as they continue to try to outdo each other, it's our gain. Here, they use cecina (partially dried beef) rather than bistec for a concentrated beefy flavor, which goes well with their trademark salsa roja, an inky-red purée of dried chiles that's more about flavor than heat.

29. El Vilsito
Petén 248,
colonia Narvarte Poniente

Tire shop by day, taco destination by night (and that means all night; it's open until five A.M. on weekends), the open-air El Vilsito always feels like a party, as if several taqueros took over the parking lot of a drive-in diner after a drunken sock hop. Order your taco or torta with cheese here; they mix it with the meat on the grill so the cheese crisps on the edges while staying melty inside for a heavenly bite. Whatever your choice of filling—meat, nopales, or mushrooms—it's especially good with the fresh vegetables that come on a torta. Add some creamy salsa verde inside and then dab with the spicier salsa roja as you eat.

135

DEL VALLE & NARVARTE
SHOPPING

These are neighborhoods where shopping tends to be more about necessities than trinkets, but the neighborhood markets each have distinct character and specialties, and the grocery stores and niche markets seem to get better and more diverse every year.

1. Biblos
Avenida Cuauhtémoc 786,
colonia Narvarte Poniente
This is one of the city's oldest and best Middle Eastern groceries. Buy prepared foods like kibbeh, labneh, fatayer (empanadas), maamoul (date pastries), and fresh shanklish (cheese), as well as tahini, phyllo, and other core ingredients. You can even buy a hookah with guava tobacco for your Airbnb.

2. Mercado de Jamaica
Guillermo Prieto 45,
colonia Jamaica
This is the city's wholesale and retail flower market, with more than eight hundred vendors of fresh flowers, flower arrangements, live plants, and flowerpots and other accessories. Besides that, it's a good-quality market for local ingredients (perhaps because of the constant flower traffic), and there are dozens of huarache vendors in the surrounding streets.

3. Mercado Del Valle
Luz Saviñón 16,
colonia Del Valle Norte

This Sunday farmers' market offers a wide range of organic and sustainable produce, coffee, honey, chocolate, meat, fish, and practically anything else edible that is grown in the region. You can also place orders during the week to pick up at the market, since most vendors sell out early. There are also prepared foods like vegan tamales and tacos.

4. Mercado Lázaro Cárdenas Del Valle
Romero de Terreros
and Adolfo Prieto,
colonia Del Valle Norte

Being in close proximity to Roma and Condesa, this modest market has been slowly becoming more "gourmet" over the years. It's especially good for snacks and comida corrida (see page 122) at the many puestos (see page 56). Recommended: Las

Margaritas, Quesadillas Doña Risa, and Café Passmar.

5. Mercado Portales
Calzada Santa Cruz
and Calle Juan Escutia,
colonia San Simón

Few of the city's almost 350 covered daily markets are truly the heart of their neighborhoods anymore, but Mercado Portales is an exception. Besides the market itself being busier than most, it extends for blocks in every direction. One distinguishing feature of this market is the many vendors of vintage and antique items, like old tortilla presses, hand-painted ceramic platters, and crystal cocktail sets.

6. Yamamoto
Avenida Porfirio Díaz 918
colonia Tlacoquemécatl Del Valle

After eating at Fonda Margarita (page 130) on the edge of Parque Tlacoquemécatl, head two blocks north to this small but jam-packed Japanese grocery store. Pro tip: Sake carafes and cups make excellent mezcal vessels.

BEYOND RESTAURANTS

Coffee Shops
Almanegra
Alquimia Café
Café Passmar
Café Vegetal
Choppeadito

Bars
Beer Bros
Cervecera
    Metropolitana
Kaito
Principia CDMX
Pulques y Curados
    "Xolo"

Bakeries
Costra
María Fortunata
Marukoshi
Pan de Nube
Sucre i Cacao

Sweets
La Frepola
Mazapanes Toledo

CANTINA LIFE

By Rulo David

Carlos Monsiváis, a superstar of Mexican literature, once described cantinas as "wayward sanctuaries in which sad, comic, tragic, melodramatic interactions abound. Every type of person meets there." The Golden Age of Mexican cinema, in the forties and fifties, portrayed cantinas as the source of everything delinquent and decadent, yet it was here where writers, artists, politicians, and academics came together to confront a changing post-Revolutionary Mexico.

Cantinas are social hubs that offer drinks, food, and chaos in equal parts; they're not places where you're likely to be booted for noise or inebriation. They have been, and continue to be, one of the few places where Mexicans of different backgrounds can coexist happily despite our varied social, professional, political, and even sports-team affinities.

Entering a cantina is like crossing a threshold into Mexico itself, to drink in the habits, passions, and idiosyncrasies of Mexicans across all social strata. But what's the difference between a cantina and a bar that serves food, or a restaurant that encourages drinking? On paper, it's virtually impossible to say; they certainly function in the same way. But they're not the same, and once you visit a few, the vague distinction starts to become clear.

Some say the difference is the quality and quantity of the botanas (see page 53), the complimentary snacks that typically come with each round of drinks—but there are cantinas that don't offer free botanas at all. Others say that cantinas are more for the masses, while restaurants and bars are for people of a higher socioeconomic level for the neighborhood—but there are pricey cantinas whose clientele are businessmen and bankers. Some hold on to the old idea that cantinas are exclusively for men to socialize—but the law prohibiting women was repealed in 1982.

What can be agreed upon is the cantina's origins in Mexico, which most historians date to the 1840s, when taverns had to serve occupying forces during the Mexican-American War. Soldiers wanted something that reminded them of home, where they could drink hard liquor without ordering food, which wasn't the norm at the time. The concept took off among locals as well. President Sebastián Lerdo de Tejada started issuing specific cantina licenses in 1872, and by century's end there were more than one thousand licensed cantinas in Mexico City alone. Unlike pulquerías, which only served pulque and were considered somewhat seedy, cantinas—as they do today—ranged from divey bars to luxe meeting places, for all classes of people, even though women (and policemen) weren't admitted until much later.

The first cantina in Mexico City was El Nivel, which had license 0001 until it closed in 2008. La Peninsular and **El Gallo de Oro** (page 36) are likely the oldest still in operation, founded, respectively, in 1872 and 1874 and still going strong in the Centro Histórico. Another vintage cantina still in operation is **La Ópera**, founded in 1876, an elegant establishment with art deco decor sourced from Spain, and where it's presumed that the bullet hole still visible in the ceiling was left by Pancho Villa during the Revolution. Historic cantinas like this allow you to sit where Fidel Castro and Che Guevara once bonded over Marxism (at **La Potosina**), or where William S. Burroughs and Jack Kerouac sought inspiration (**Tío Pepe** was a favorite during their time in the city).

Cantina food—la comida cantinera—is usually a mix of traditional Mexican and Spanish dishes. On the Mexican side, you'll find caldo de camarón (shrimp broth), chamorro (whole pork shank), milanesa (pork or chicken cutlets), fried fish filets or salt-crusted whole fish, chicharrón (pork rinds) en salsa verde, shrimp cocktail, or beef tartare. On the Spanish side, look for chistorra

(semi-cured sausage) in cider or white wine, Galician-style octopus, croquettes, tortilla española, paella, or fabada. Most have specialties, like tribilin (a ceviche of raw beef, fish, and shrimp) at **El Mirador de Chapultepec** (page 15), ate con queso flameado (crisp grilled cheese with guava paste) at **Bar El Sella** (page 11), or the caracoles (snails in mole sauce) at **El Dux de Venecia**.

Some cantinas also have live music or, failing that, let street musicians roam table to table offering pay-per-song services. There's no better setting for these musicians than a cantina, as the mariachi repertoire mostly comprises drink-friendly songs about romance, bravery, death, and patriotism.

Cantina-centric classics like "Mil cantinas," "Cantina de mi barrio," and "El cantinero" mostly have to do with drowning sorrows; the saddest lament of all, "Borracho sin cantina," has the singer asking that the cantina door be his burial ground.

It's this interconnection with Mexican daily life that helps explain why cantinas not only have survived the passage of time but continue to be extremely popular, despite the emergence of sports bars, cocktail bars, mezcalerías, and everywhere else people drink. Amid the inevitable gentrification that's moving at breakneck speed throughout the city, they are sanctuaries. See where to find these great cantinas, and discover even more, below.

OUR FAVORITE CANTINAS:

Bar El Sella
Dr. Balmis 210, colonia Doctores
One of the few cantinas known specifically for its food, this is a jewel of colonia Doctores (page 11).

Cantina El Bosque
13 de Septiembre 29,
colonia San Miguel Chapultepec
Looking for a late-afternoon party? Be sure to bring change for the roving musicians (page 11).

El Dux de Venecia
Avenida Azcapotzalco 586A,
colonia Centro de Azcapotzalco

La Faena
Venustiano Carranza 49, Centro Histórico
This lost-in-time cantina doubles as a bullfighting museum (page 35).

El Gallo de Oro
Venustiano Carranza 35, Centro Histórico
Opened in 1874, this is one of the country's oldest cantinas (page 36).

El Golfo de León
Joaquín Velázquez de León 79,
colonia San Rafael
In a neighborhood with several of them, this is an archetypal classic cantina (page 65).

El Mirador de Chapultepec
Avenida Chapultepec 606,
colonia San Miguel Chapultepec
Try the tribilin, which is, essentially, a fish and shrimp ceviche with cubes of raw beef added (page 15).

La Ópera
Avenida 5 de Mayo 10, Centro Histórico

La Potosina
Jesús María 21, Centro Histórico

Salón Familiar La Mascota
Mesones 20, Centro Histórico
Come for generous—and tasty—botanas (see page 53); just be ready for a three-drink minimum before they start coming gratis (page 38).

Salón París
Jaime Torres Bodet 151,
colonia Santa María la Ribera
Now in a new(ish) location across the street from its original location, this popular afternoon spot retains its boozy, singalong old-school vibe (page 66).

Tío Pepe
Avenida Independencia 26, Centro Histórico

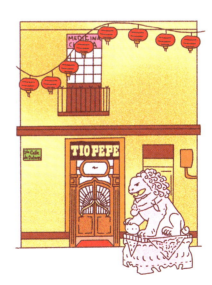

141

HOTELS WITH THE BEST FOOD BUILT IN

The boom in Mexico City tourism has shifted the city's luxury hotels away from corporate high-rises for business travelers, toward a wider range of more intimate and culturally minded boutique offerings. At the same time, the corporate palaces have become more attuned to the importance of food and drink in a city where that is a primary draw. Besides having especially unique or varied food and drink offerings on site, these hotels are located in areas known for great food.

Āgata Hotel Boutique & Spa

Avenida México 21,
colonia Del Carmen, Coyoacán

A smart choice if you want to stay in charming Coyoacán (page 106), this homey four-room residence also offers several cooking classes and tastings that are more like eating classes (i.e., you get to the good part quicker). Particularly recommended is the private Alta Cocina Mexicana experience, where you can choose from your choice of appetizer, entrée, and dessert. The (included) breakfasts are particularly good, and they also work with the tour group The Trusty Compass to book customized food-related tours.

Casona

Durango 280, colonia Roma Norte

This lovingly restored 1923 mansion is one of only a few dozen buildings in the city officially designated as "artistic monuments." With only thirty-two rooms, it has several food and drink options that non-guests should consider as well. Celeb chef Aquiles Chávez helms two concepts: Aquiles, which serves impeccable versions of Mexican classics in an elegant setting, and Suchi, which combines Japanese techniques and presentation with the seafood-based cuisine of Sinaloa state in northern Mexico. Akamba is an "agave gallery" that has a huge selection of Mexican spirits and offers guided tastings. La Macaria is a tea room centered around matcha, with delicious pastries made in-house. Don't miss afternoon cocktails on the tree-ringed rooftop.

InterContinental Presidente

Campos Elíseos 218, colonia Polanco

Though a corporate chain hotel, this Polanco icon is an important part of CDMX architectural history. Built between 1969 and 1977, the hotel was once the tallest hotel in Latin America and the tallest concrete building in the world. Today, the forty-two-story skyscraper boasts eight restaurants of all stripes. Au Pied de Cochon is the only fine-dining restaurant in the city open twenty-four hours, with classic French cuisine and a lengthy wine list. There's a branch of NYC steakhouse the Palm, a Japanese sushi-and-cocktail bar, an Italian spot called Alfredo di Roma with a textbook eponymous fettuccine Alfredo, a gin-and-tonic bar that also has sixty-six tequila brands, and yes, Mexican food, too, at the Oaxacan-inspired Chapulín, named after that state's edible grasshoppers. The hotel is also near Quintonil (page 86), Pujol (page 86), and the many restaurants and bars surrounding lovely Parque Lincoln.

St. Regis

Avenida Paseo de la Reforma 439, colonia Cuauhtémoc

Choose from several fun dining spots at this luxe hotel (the smallest rooms are more than five hundred square feet) located three blocks from Chapultepec Park. Start with a drink at the King Cole Bar overlooking the iconic Ángel de la Independencia monument. Choose omakase at Sushi Tatsugoro from the acclaimed Edo Kobayashi group, or La Table Krug, a private eight-course dining experience paired with Krug Champagne. The flagship Restaurante Diana has a broad menu with creative Mexican dishes like pork belly–stuffed squid with Yucatecan recado negro, and duck flautas in mole from Xico, Veracruz.

For celebrities, romantics, or special occasions, private meals can be arranged twenty-four hours a day, either in-room or in discreet private dining spaces.

La Valise

Tonalá 53, colonia Roma Norte

Each of the eight suites at colonia Roma's worst-kept secret is the apartment of your dreams, with art, antiques, and collectibles that give each one a unique personality. Here you can pretend that the city's best restaurants are your private chefs. Rather than one in-house restaurant, the hotel has contracted with several of the city's top restaurants to deliver in-room service. At no other hotel is so much of the city's best dining accessible with one call to the concierge.

143

20 de Noviembre
Centro de
 Azcapotzalco
Clavería
Guadalupe
 Insurgentes
Hogar y Seguridad
Industrial
Industrial Vallejo
Industrias Tulpetlac
La Preciosa
Lindavista
Nueva Industrial
 Vallejo
Nueva Santa María

Nueva Vallejo
Peralvillo
Porvenir
San Andrés
San Bartolo
 Atepehuacan
Santa Rosa
Tepeyac
 Insurgentes
Vallejo Poniente
Venustiano
 Carranza
Victoria de las
 Democracias

7

RTH

AVE. ACUEDUCTO

13 **1**

SANTA ROSA

AUTOP. NAUCALPAN – ECATEPEC

EJE CENTRAL LÁZARO CÁRDENAS

NUEVA
INDUSTRIAL
VALLEJO

23

LINDAVISTA

18

SAN ANDRÉS

15

AVE. CEYLAN

CALZADA VALLEJO

INDUSTRIAL
VALLEJO

5

SAN BARTOLO
ATEPEHUACAN

AV. INSTITUTO POLITECNICO NACIONAL

NUEVA
VALLEJO

3

AV. MONTEVID.

25

TEPEYAC
INSURGENTES

7

14
1

LA
PRECIOSA

AVE. DE LAS GRANJAS

CENTRO
DE
AZCAPOTZALCO

11

20 **21**
16

19

INDUSTRI

HOGAR Y
SEGURIDAD

GUADALUPE
INSURGENTES

PORVENIR

VALLEJO
PONIENTE

26

8

6

12

17

VICTORIA DE
LAS DEMOCRACIAS

2

CLAVERÍA

NUEVA
SANTA MARÍA

AV. INSURGENTES NTE.

27

2

PERALVILLO

AV. DE LOS MISTERIOS

20 DE
NOVIEMBRE

NORTH

DINING

1. Antojitos Daniela
2. Antojitos La Torre
3. Birria la Jalisciense
4. Caldos de Gallina "El Porvenir"
5. El Camaroncito Loco
6. Casa de Toño (La Original)
7. Casa Don Juve
8. Frutería y Lonchería Ojo de Agua
9. Gorditas Ahogadas El Güero
10. Kimchi
11. Mariscos Don Panchito
12. Nicos
13. Pancita Don Poncho
14. La Perla Tapatía
15. Petroleras de "La Güera"
16. Pozolería Jalisco
17. Pulquería La Reforma de las Carambolas
18. Quesadillas Díaz
19. El Rebaño Sagrado
20. El Sabalito
21. Tacos El Buen Tono
22. Taquería Javier
23. Taquería Las Torres
24. Taquería y Parrillada "El Güero"
25. Tlacoyos La Manita
26. Tortas de Vallejo
27. TzinTzunTzan

SHOPPING

1. Mercado Azcapotzalco
2. Mercado Nueva Santa María

NORTH
DINING

The two northernmost of Mexico City's sixteen delegaciones (boroughs)—
Azcapotzalco and Gustavo A. Madero—are home to more than one and a half
million of the city's residents but remain virtually unknown to most tourists.
Though the Basílica de Santa María de Guadalupe, located in Gustavo A.
Madero, is one of the city's crown jewels and the most visited Catholic shrine
in the world, few of its twenty million annual pilgrims explore much beyond the
sprawling complex. As for Azcapotzalco, most gastro-minded visitors know it
for the restaurant Nicos (page 151), which is often mentioned with caveats of
its being "far," even though the twenty-minute ride from Chapultepec Park is
shorter than it usually takes to traverse the length of colonia Roma.

    Restaurants in this part of the city are mostly straightforward spots for
service workers (accordingly, there is relatively little open at night, considering
how many people live here). Yet this being Mexico City, many of these low-key
spots can be revelatory. Pair a culinary ramble with a visit to one of the area's many
attractions: Monumento a la Raza, Azcapotzalco Museum, San Juan de Aragón
Zoo, the seventeen-hectare Tezozómoc Park, a concert or game at the twenty-
two-thousand-capacity Arena CDMX, or Acuario Michín, the country's largest
aquarium, which opened in October 2023. With urban action, historic charm, and
ample nature, a day in the north is a pleasant escape from the tourist hordes in the
central neighborhoods.

1. Antojitos Daniela
Calle 28-A, 51,
colonia Santa Rosa

Don't let the vast menu throw you; the specialty here is huaraches (see page 42), made of fresh masa patted into huge thin ovals, griddled until the edges crisp up but the centers stay tender. They come smeared with beans, salsa, raw onion, and finely crumbled cheese, then your choice of toppings, from nopales (cactus paddles) to pork rib to chewy skirt steak (if you're there for breakfast, try it with a couple of fried eggs). No matter the time of day, their café de olla (coffee brewed with unrefined sugar and Mexican cinnamon) is essential.

2. Antojitos La Torre
Beethoven 212,
colonia Peralvillo

Near the San Joaquín market is the busiest gordita spot in the neighborhood, dating back to 1964. Here the corn masa is ground with fresh corn kernels, providing incredible texture and flavor when fried. Everyone orders them filled with chicharrón (pork rinds), but ask for a fried egg as well—the yolk-soaked chicharrón makes for one of the most glorious bites in the city. Order a glass of tepache (see page 57) for a perfect pairing.

3. Birria la Jalisciense
Avenida Montevideo 518,
colonia San Bartolo
Atepehuacan

If cheap beer, loud ranchero music, and bone marrow sound like a good time, this is your place. Although the specialty is birria (get it "tatemado," charred and crisped so the flavors concentrate), your first order has to be the bone marrow taco, a just-made tortilla heaped with hot marrow to which you add a little salt and chipotle salsa. Or try the "plato especial," a platter with chicharrón (pork rinds), pickled nopales, avocado, tomato, panela cheese, and tortillas, to make "tacos placeros," a mix of all the above. Don't leave without trying the pecan pulque (see page 51).

4. Caldos de Gallina "El Porvenir"
Herreros and Tipografía 118,
colonia Venustiano Carranza

Caldo de gallina—chicken soup—is a known healer, whether your malady is a mild cold or just some overindulgence the night before, so this soup spot is especially popular on weekends. The servings here are hearty and flavorful, but save room for the enchiladas, too. The salsa-soaked tortillas come with green or mole sauce and are filled with your choice of chicken, pork rib,

or egg. An order of red rice and a bolillo (roll) help to wipe the plate clean.

5. El Camaroncito Loco
Norte 45 1071,
Industrial Vallejo

The food court in the Price Shoes shopping complex hardly screams "lunch destination," but El Camaroncito Loco (the Crazy Little Shrimp) stands out for its attention to detail. Here you'll find fried fish filets that look imported from a UK fish-and-chips shop, breaded jumbo shrimp, and ceviches made fresh throughout the day. The fried fish and shrimp empanadas are modeled after the ones served to workers at La Nueva Viga (see page 157), the city's wholesale fish market, split while hot and gilded with mayonnaise, lime, and bottled Valentina salsa. Since there's no booze, get the virgin piña colada if they have it.

6. Casa de Toño (La Original)

Calle Floresta 77, colonia Clavería

This is the original location of one of the most successful chains in all Chilangolandia. What began in a family home in the seventies is now an empire, but is still beloved by most for its unwavering hospitality and tasty comfort food. Pozole is a must-order (there's a vegetarian option made with squash blossom); follow it with flautas of shredded beef covered in crema, queso fresco, and a shower of lettuce. To drink, try the Toma Toño, their house-made clamato with beer.

7. Casa Don Juve

Calle San Mateo 90, colonia La Preciosa

For octopus fans, this slender 1940s cantina is worth the trip just for its torta de pulpo, a sandwich stuffed with octopus braised in its jet-black ink (the octopus can also be ordered as a main dish without the bread). Pad your meal with other dishes like a thick lentil soup with bacon and garlic-smothered quail, and wash it down with a cold beer, Cuba libre, or any of the two pages of drinks (that's how you know it's a cantina and not a simple café).

8. Frutería y Lonchería Ojo de Agua

Clave 444, colonia Vallejo Poniente

Curiously, this place has no relation to the (very good) Ojo de Agua chain that has countless locations across Mexico, though it shares a commitment to fresh produce, juices, and healthy but hearty breakfasts. At first glance it looks like a fruit stand, but in the back, you'll find some tables and a bar to place your order. Any of the fresh juices and aguas frescas are excellent, but for breakfast (or, really, anytime) be sure to also get the chilaquiles en salsa verde. The tortillas stay crunchy even when drenched in the sauce, which has a salivating acidity that has you going back for bite after bite. Best of all? It's open twenty-four hours a day, seven days a week.

9. Gorditas El Güero

Mercado Industrias Tulpetlec, Locale 48 (across the street from Avenida Europa 243), colonia Industrias Tulpetlac

It may take a minute to locate this spot among the many market stands at the same address, but it's worth the hunt. You've heard of tortas ahogadas (sandwiches drenched in a brothy tomato-chile salsa), maybe even flautas ahogadas, but you need to try these habit-forming little gorditas ahogadas. Thick tortillas are fried, split, and filled with stewed pork rinds, raw onion, and cilantro. They're bathed in salsa just before serving, so you just need a squeeze of lime before digging in. Order three for a satisfying lunch, paired with ice-cold tamarind Jarritos.

10. Kimchi

Avenida Ricarte 41, Guadalupe Insurgentes
colonia Tepeyac Insurgentes
This modest Korean gem could easily hold its own in the competitive restaurant scene of Roma, Condesa, or Juárez. Try the ramyeon (noodles), which come flavored with kimchi or a spicy gochujang-based sauce, the little gamja hot dogs (Korean corn dogs), or the popular kimchi bokkeumbab (fried rice) topped with a fried egg. Weekends feature Korean sweet-and-spicy fried chicken. This is a good choice for before or after a visit to the Basílica de Santa María de Guadalupe.

11. Mariscos Don Panchito

Poniente 122 and Norte 19, colonia Nueva Vallejo
This seafood restaurant takes up the first two floors of a cheery orange neighborhood home, and the atmosphere is appropriately familial. This isn't a place for austere aguachiles and dainty oysters on the half shell. Start with an order of pescadillas (fried quesadillas [page 56] with shredded fish), followed by toritos (jalapeños stuffed with shrimp and cheese), a shrimp cocktail with or without ketchup (without is "a la marinera") and finish with a whole fried mojarra (tilapia) that's perfect for two to share. Wash it down with beers or fresh horchata.

12. Nicos

Avenida Cuitláhuac 3102, colonia Clavería
Nicos's multitude of awards is a testament to its quality but belies its homey appeal. It was one of the first restaurants in the city to turn a neighborhood fonda (see page 56) into a destination, a slow-food temple of local ingredients and rare, often historic recipes (not to mention the first all-Mexican wine list). Current chef-owner Gerardo Vázquez Lugo inherited Nicos from his parents, and for all its refinement, his main accomplishment is carrying on their legacy, making it a beautifully reliable neighborhood restaurant that celebrates Mexico's remarkable culinary history without pretense.

13. Pancita Don Poncho

Avenida 1-A 53, colonia Santa Rosa
It's open every day (though just until 2:45 P.M.), but Don Poncho is more fun on the weekends, when mariachi trios stroll by, there's a balloon vendor who looks as if he'll go airborne at any minute, and you're most likely to need this favorite hangover cure. The pancita (aka menudo, a hearty beef tripe broth), already richly seasoned with chile and oregano, comes with fresh tortillas, onion, salsas, and lime. There are two

sizes—traditional (large) and small (still pretty big)—and if you finish the traditional, they give you a free refill with some of the bones used to flavor the broth. The only downside is the perpetual line, though it rarely exceeds twenty minutes.

14. La Perla Tapatía
Avenida Azcapotzalco 706-B, colonia Centro de Azcapotzalco
Jalisco-style birria (chile-braised meat) is the order at this popular spot ("tapatía" is the adjective for being from Jalisco), served on a platter with huge fresh tortillas. Ask for the onions and spicy salsa on the side so you can taquear (make the tacos yourself). Finish with a cold beer and an order of jericalla, the typical flan of Jalisco.

15. Petroleras de "La Güera"
Cedros 73, colonia San Andres
Petroleras are the classic antojito of northern Mexico City, specifically Azcapotzalco, and these are probably the most famous of them all. A petrolera is a large, thick round tortilla

(something like a round huarache), cooked dry on the comal or fried in oil (here they're fried) and topped like a pizza. Beans, salsa, cheese, cream, and lettuce are a given, then choose your guisado (prepared topping): chicharrón (pork rinds), beef picadillo, chicken, mushroom, or egg. You can also get half and half.

16. Pozolería Jalisco
Avenida la Fortuna 100, colonia Tepeyac Insurgentes
Being a pozole restaurant by name, this place mostly lures pozole fans choosing from small, medium, and large pozole servings with surtida (mixed pork cuts), maciza (lean cuts only), chicken, or vegetarian. Another option, though, is to go rogue and order birria or the many grilled meats—pork chops, chicken breast, Argentine chorizo (see page 55), several cuts of beef—that are a bargain when compared to nearby steakhouses or Argentinian restaurants.

17. Pulquería La Reforma de las Carambolas
Yerbabuena 65, colonia Victoria de las Democracias
This rustic open-air pulquería has been in the Vázquez Ayala family for more than eighty years and became famous in pulque circles for the curado de

jitomate, or pulque flavored with fresh tomato, which other pulquerías soon replicated. Other popular flavors include guava, pine nut, pistachio, and oatmeal, but try the natural—plain—to appreciate the freshness compared to some other pulquerías in the city. The botana (see page 53), offered free as you drink, is a chicharrón (pork rind) taco with an exceptionally spicy sauce that the pulque readily quenches.

18. Quesadillas Díaz
Poniente 150 and Norte 59, Industrial Vallejo
In an industrial area somewhat between the Instituto Politécnico Nacional (one of the country's largest universities) and Arena CDMX (a twenty-thousand-capacity sports and concert venue) is this blink-and-you'll-miss-it stand that starts serving workers at seven A.M. until it runs out of food (usually around two or three in the afternoon). The quesadillas de tinga (shredded chicken in a smoky tomato sauce) are the draw here, served with queso fresco and onion and cooked on the comal with a bit of fat so the edges have a little crunch. Owner Doña María also makes tacos dorados (fried) of whatever she has that day, such as potatoes with chorizo (see page 55). The salsa verde is especially good,

with tiny bits of minced fresh green chile.

19. El Rebaño Sagrado

Necaxa #232,
colonia Guadalupe Insurgentes

Open from nine A.M. to midnight (with a lunch break from three to five), this destination is kind of like two taquerías in one: In the daytime, it's all about birria. At night, it's a tacos de fritanga (see page 119) spot where the popular cuts are suadero (see page 57), cabeza, lengua (tongue), and tripas (see page 57). Get the tripas cooked "doradito" (well fried) and all with plenty of the red salsa, which is more about flavor than heat. Tortillas are swiped through the residual meat fat on the comal for an extra-delicious touch.

20. El Sabalito

Avenida la Fortuna 197,
colonia Tepeyac Insurgentes

What this friendly (to your stomach and your wallet)

Sinaloan-style seafood spot lacks in atmosphere, it more than makes up for on the plate. Start with an oyster-clamato shot and a shrimp aguachile (see page 53) tostada, follow with toritos (which here are jalapeños stuffed with shredded marlin and cheese), and then fish filets cooked either with mojo de ajo or empapelado (en papillote) with tomato, onion, and cilantro.

21. Tacos El Buen Tono

Avenida la Fortuna 130,
colonia Tepeyac Insurgentes

This is a true taco institution in the Tepeyac Insurgentes neighborhood, famed for its suadero tacos (see page 57) and late-night crowds (it's open until two A.M. daily). The tongue tacos are equally delicious, begging to be eaten with spicy salsa roja and extra lime, and the tacos al pastor can be griddled crisp if you ask nicely. Get everything with grilled spring onions and nopales on the side.

22. Taquería Javier

Mercado Octavio Senties Gómez-Local 13-35,
colonia 20 de Noviembre

Inside the Octavio Senties market are some of the tastiest tripas (small intestine) tacos around. You can order it crispy or soft, and tacos are accompanied by a tasty salsa roja of cooked tomatillos and chile de árbol. Try it with grilled potato and onion, or skip the tripas and just get a taco campechano (mixed) of bistec and longaniza. It's a smart stop in a less-visited neighborhood and across from a lovely church, Parroquia de Nuestra Señora de San Juan de los Lagos.

23. Taquería Las Torres

Frente Plaza Torres, Lindavista,
Nueva Industrial Vallejo

This stand sits across from a Vips (think Denny's), like David facing Goliath and knowing full well the win is his. The specialty here is organ meats: hígado (liver), riñón (kidney), and machitos (a mix of innards), as well as a particularly flavorful longaniza. They are among the biggest tacos in town, debunking the idea that taco fillings should nestle neatly inside the tortilla: The meat quantity here could easily stuff a torta, and the tacos are further fortified with griddle-fried potatoes and long-cooked strips of jalapeño and onion. One will do the trick.

153

24. Taquería y Parrillada "El Güero"

Laminadores 45,
colonia 20 de Noviembre

This is one of the oldest and most beloved taquerías in the neighborhood, where the servings are large enough to make multiple tacos from one platter of meat. One of the more unusual specialties here is suadero (see page 57) with cheese. The cheese might seem like overkill with the fatty meat, but the leagues of loyal customers disagree. The richness is mitigated by a dish of cucumbers with lime, cactus, and pápalo, a vaguely anise-flavored herb whose bracing freshness is just what you need to keep munching.

25. Tlacoyos La Manita

Lindavista and Chiclayo, Parque Deportivo Miguel Alemán colonia Lindavista Norte

There are many stands hoping to serve those working up an appetite at the soccer, baseball, basketball, and tennis courts in Parque Deportivo Miguel Alemán, but since 1988, the long-standing favorite has been this steaming comal full of blue corn delights. The specialty is the longaniza quesadilla, with sausage the owner brings from the town of Xalatlaco (a ninety-minute drive southwest), seasoned richly with bright guajillo chile and earthy achiote. Also not to be missed are quelites (wild greens) cooked with onion until wilted and tender. There are also freshly formed tlacoyos (filled oval tortillas; see page 43) of fresh requesón (a ricotta-like cheese) or crushed fava beans.

26. Tortas de Vallejo

Calle 7 167,
colonia Porvenir

Most know this street stand simply as "Ricas Tortas Gigantes," a phrase decoratively painted all over the exterior, and a bold statement in a torta-crazed city like this one. Though all the tortas are tasty, locals come for the lengua, which here features thin-sliced pork tongue (milder than the more common beef tongue) confited in lard and piled high on a roll with avocado and pickled chiles (shown above). If tongue isn't your thing, the milanesa de pollo (pounded and griddled chicken) wins the silver medal for popularity.

27. TzinTzunTzan

Franz Schubert 210-Interior 80, colonia Peralvillo

Taquero Don Alfredo took the name from his hometown of Tzintzuntzan, in Michoacán state. Alfredo's star taco is barbacoa de res (see page 116), which in this case is cabeza (beef head), cooked with agave leaves that lend a subtly smoky touch. He piles the meat on just-cooked tortillas, adds some very spicy guacamole (for less heat, skip the guac), then tops it with another tortilla so the heat doesn't escape. Accompany your taco with a cup of beef broth, bulked up with garbanzos and rice. If you eat ten (you won't), your order is free!

NORTH
SHOPPING

This is a large, spread-out, not particularly walkable area, and a tricky pick for a shopping adventure. That said, being off the tourist track, north can be a treat for bargain hunters, especially those who don't mind a dearth of designer boutiques or cutting-edge art.

1. Mercado Azcapotzalco
Esperanza 357,
colonia Centro de Azcapotzalco,
Azcapotzalco

This cheery market was constructed in the 1950s and remodeled in 2020, and today it has a nice combination of tradition and modernity, with sleek, wide corridors giving easy access to more than five hundred vendors. Though it's rarely visited by tourists, it remains an important commercial hub of this revitalized area, and hasn't suffered from the loss of daily patronage that's affected so many other of the city's neighborhood markets. Besides the usual array of fruits, vegetables, meat, and fish, there's also clothing, kitchenware, crafts, and dozens of vendors selling spiritual wares like rare herbs, candles, amulets, potions, and dolls.

2. Mercado Nueva Santa María
Vid 169,
colonia Nueva Santa María,
Azcapotzalco

If you have kids, keep this market in mind. Here, the young and young at heart can roam the many toy sellers that are among its almost 250 vendors, where you can also shop for fresh produce and food souvenirs like small-batch salsas and sticks of canela (Mexican cinnamon) longer than your arm. There's little else that distinguishes it from other neighborhood markets, but it's a nice choice when you need to get away from the English-speaking hordes. A block away is the gorgeous, peaceful Parque Revolución, which boasts several mature árboles de ahuehuete, aka Montezuma cypress, Mexico's national tree.

BEYOND RESTAURANTS

Coffee Shops
Apolo Café
Café Once28
Obertura Café

Bars
El Dux de Venecia
Monasterio de las
    Cervezas
Pulquería La Puerta
    Verde
Pulquería La Xula

Bakeries
Centteno Panadería
    Artesanal
Flor de María
    Panadería
Panadería y Pastelería
    Tierra Nueva

Sweets
Bremen
Dulce Andar
Meyvi Helados
    Lindavista
Paletería y Nevería
    La Estrella

SPOTLIGHT: SEAFOOD

The hottest place to be in Mexico City at four A.M. isn't at some Condesa afterparty, but in the borough of Iztapalapa in the east end of the city, where thousands of buyers and sellers converge before sunrise in the wholesale fish market **La Nueva Viga**. It's a must-visit for any seafood-loving early risers, not to stock your fridge but to bear witness to the city's greatest food-related spectacle, one that few tourists (or locals, for that matter) ever see.

La Nueva Viga is the second-largest fish market in the world by volume, second only to Tokyo's famed Toyosu Market. Roughly 60 percent of Mexico's seafood, coming from all its many coasts, passes through here, to be sold not just in Mexico City and the surrounding regions but to the rest of the country as well. As a

result, in many cases, fish caught just off coastal cities come to Mexico City before going right back where they came from.

But with the nearest port about 250 miles away, why is it all sent to this landlocked capital? Some say it can be traced back to Moctezuma II, the ruler of the Aztec empire in the early sixteenth century, just before the Spanish conquests. To satisfy his enormous demands, elaborate trade routes were established, which later became a formal trade network that established Mexico City as the commercial hub of New Spain. Demand plays a role as well: With the Mexico City metropolitan area and the surrounding State of Mexico comprising more than a quarter of the country's population, it's by far the largest market for commercial fisheries.

No other city so far inland has seafood as fresh and varied as Mexico City. Take note of its omnipresence as you explore the city: Ceviches, aguachiles (see page 53), and shellfish cocktails are as ubiquitous here as burgers and pizza in the United States. Lesser-known items like abalone, geoduck, langoustines, barnacles, and pata de mula (blood clams) are served everywhere from market stalls to fine-dining restaurants. There's every style of grilled and braised fish imaginable, often cloaked in herby green moles and nutty pipianes, or a la veracruzana with olives and capers. Salt-crusted whole fish is a popular entrée in upscale cantinas, where people also order caldo de camarón (shrimp broth) as a hangover helper. Octopus shows up raw, grilled, and stewed. The seafood-based cuisine of coastal Sinaloa has exploded in Mexico City, and there is world-class sushi made exclusively with Mexican fish. Contramar's (page 13) iconic tuna tostadas are found in hundreds of restaurants, few as good as the original, but all with sashimi-grade tuna.

A visit to La Nueva Viga is key to appreciating the sheer freshness and abundance of Mexico City's seafood scene. The market opens at three A.M., when the first daily shipments arrive and buyers start haggling over six-foot bluefin tuna while literal tons of shrimp are sorted into dozens of species as live crabs and lobsters flail futilely. Most vendors stay until early afternoon, but if you want to see the action, go early, as most major commerce is done by nine A.M., which is also when most of the market's sit-down restaurants open. It's fun to watch vendors, who have been working all night, sitting down at mid-morning with plates of raw clams, ceviche tostadas, and whole grilled fish, with beers and even mezcal. Tip: Wear waterproof boots to protect against the canals of melting ice, fish blood, and seawater that flow through the crowded corridors.

There are dozens of stands all over the market serving things like pescadillas (fish quesadillas), empanadas, and fried mojarra (a tilapia relative) to workers on the move. These sit-down restaurants are at the southeastern edge of the market, opening daily around nine A.M. The places below share an address with the market's main building.

El Erizo Loco

There's not always the namesake erizo at "The Crazy Sea Urchin" (get it, if they have it), but this cheery, generous spot has some less-seen dishes like caguamanta (a northern Mexican stew of ray wings), Peruvian-style ceviches, and a choice of lobsters from Mexico's Pacific or Caribbean coasts.

La Matoza

La Matoza has served market workers since 1955, and its breezy, minimalist space is a nice respite from the market's chaos when it opens at nine A.M. The menu spans every preparation imaginable, but try the shareable vuelve a la vida cocktail with eight types of seafood.

El Puerto de Alvarado

This is a good choice if you want to start the day on a healthy note, with generous fish salads and breakfast dishes of eggs with shellfish and veggies. Still, you'll be tempted by a variety of fish cooked thirteen ways and octopus seven ways; try whole róbalo (sea bass), huachinango (red snapper), or mojarra prepared al ajillo, with guajillo chile and tons of garlic.

La Nueva Viga

Eje 6 Sur 560, Área Federal Central de Abastos, Iztapalapa

THREE CHILANGO-APPROVED OVERNIGHT TRIPS

By **Liliana López Sorzano**

There's more cuisine and culture contained within the sprawling borders of Mexico City than could be experienced over an entire lifetime. And yet, the city is also a hub, a central lily pad from which travelers leap to any number of Mexico's other states and attractions, from its peaceful beaches to its varied urban and cultural centers. Locals, too, venture out, seeking a break from all the stimulation from time to time. Here, then, are the favorite quick escapes of three notable chilangos.

TRIP 1: Tepoztlán

by Gabriela Cámara

No trip to Mexico City is complete without a trip to Contramar (page 13), the seafood-focused playground of chef, restaurateur, and bona fide culinary celebrity Gabriela Cámara. While Contramar may have been inspired by Mexico's Pacific coast, Cámara spent her childhood in Tepoztlán, a small town about an hour's drive from Mexico City in the landlocked state of Morelos.

"To this day, Tepoztlán is the place where the family gathers to celebrate a special occasion," says Cámara. In Tepoztlán, the tranquil feel is bolstered by the town's iconic landmark, El Tepozteco, an ancient Aztec temple and pyramid situated at the top of Tepozteco Mountain. Tourists and hikers come here to climb its steps and soak in the panoramic views of the surrounding area. A new crop of boutique hotels and restaurants have opened in the past few years as well, making the town a great weekend getaway for travelers in search of natural beauty as well as culinary delights. Check out Cámara's favorite spots to eat, play, and relax in Tepoztlán.

For a meal with a mission

Parcela is a new place with ambitions that go far beyond those of just a restaurant. The owners have created an organic and regenerative garden, which we work with to grow many of the vegetables that we use in the restaurants. Visiting the farm is a great way to spend the morning. They offer high-quality farm-to-table seasonal products and host various workshops for groups, from bird-watching to watercolor painting.

Parcela
Avenida Ignacio Zaragoza 408, Tepoztlán

For a traditional breakfast or lunch

When the family gets together, we like to go to the **El Ciruelo** hotel for breakfast. It's a peaceful place with a great view of the Tepozteco, and the restaurant's menu offers traditional dishes from all over Mexico. I like to order chilaquiles with cecina (dried beef) or scrambled eggs with vegetables and salsa tatemada (charred salsa).

El Ciruelo
Avenida Ignacio Zaragoza 17, Tepoztlán

For views

Whenever I have friends visiting for the first time, I always suggest they hike to the top of **Tepozteco Mountain,** where there's a pyramid built between 1200 and 1300 CE, six hundred meters above the Tepoztlán Valley. According to archaeologists, these ruins were part of a small architectural complex built during the rule of Ahuízotl of Tenochtitlan.

The moderate hike to Tepozteco can take between 90 and 120 minutes.

El Tepozteco
Carretera Federal libre, Cuernavaca, Tepoztlán

Where to shop and snack

I love to recommend eating and shopping for handicrafts at the **Mercado Organico de Tepoztlán**. While there, I like to stop at any of the quesadilla stands, or I'll get some mole enchiladas at **Axitla**, where Laura, the cook and owner, makes the same delicious red mole recipe that her mother used to make at La Tapatia, one of the first restaurants for foreign visitors in Tepoztlán. My father, Gabriel, used to go there with his cousin the poet Carlos Pellicer Cámara in the early forties, back when there wasn't even a road.

Mercado Orgánico de Tepoztlán
Santo Domingo Tepoztlán

Axitla
Del Tepozteco, Tierra Blanca, Tepoztlán

Where to stay

I stay at the family house whenever I go to Tepoztlán, but I always suggest that friends stay at **Amomoxtli Spa and Hotel**, or at least eat at the restaurant. I especially like the spa because it offers a blend of experienced therapists and ancestral techniques to recover and pamper the body. It's fun to check out its bar, library, terrace, and living room, which provide a homey place to relax.

Amomoxtli Spa and Hotel
Matamoros Extension 115, Tepoztlán

TRIP 2:
Oaxaca

by Enrique Olvera

Via his slate of acclaimed restaurants spread throughout North America, chef Enrique Olvera has become one of the world's foremost ambassadors for Mexican gastronomy. Pujol (page 86), his flagship fine-dining restaurant in Mexico City, will soon celebrate its twenty-fifth anniversary, and his US portfolio includes restaurants like Cosme and Atla in New York and Damian and Ditroit Taquería in LA, and there are even more openings on the horizon.

But of all the places his career has taken him, Oaxaca—known for its complex cuisine, colonial architecture, and rich tradition of mezcal making—is the one he finds himself returning to again and again. "The first time I went to Oaxaca was when I was eleven years old, with my parents," says Olvera. "It made a very strong impression on me, because of the strength of the colors and the intensity of the flavors of food. I think that intensity refers to the depth in which things are done here."

Olvera began traveling to Oaxaca more regularly starting in 2004, he says, "where I would meet traditional cooks and stop at markets, production facilities, and traditional food places." Oaxaca has since become fundamental to Pujol's tasting menu—"Just think of the moles," he says. "Our approach to Mexican cuisine had always been through street food [e.g., tacos], but we had never gotten into this kind of regional or ceremonial cuisine before." Through Oaxaca, he says, the menu found its ancestral roots. Here, then, are Olvera's favorite places to experience Oaxaca.

For lunch

I usually go to **Alfonsina** for lunch right after I have landed, because it's on the way from the airport to the city. I like to say it's a Oaxaca custom. I love the homey vibe of the food and the place; it's as if you were invited to someone's home to eat. Jorge

León, who used to work at Pujol, and his mother, Elvia, work with what's available on the market to create the daily changing menu. I like to spend a relaxed afternoon there. Besides, they have the best tortillas in town.

Alfonsina (shown at right)
Calle García Vigil 183,
San Juan Bautista la Raya

For a snack

I like to take a stroll around Santo Domingo Square and then go to the terrace of my friend Alex Ruiz's restaurant, **Casa Oaxaca**, in the hotel of the same name. I'll eat a tlayuda with insects and pair it with a mezcalita while looking out at the church and waiting for the sunset.

Casa Oaxaca
Constitución 104-A, Ruta Independencia

For happy hour

There is a new mezcal bar called **Mistereo** that I have been visiting recently. It is a small and intimate place where they have a good selection of mezcals at good prices. **Selva** is a craft cocktail bar where I like the vibe, the music, and the ambience. After a few drinks, if I feel like eating late at night, I go to **Lechoncito de Oro**, a cart that sells lechón tacos with a spicy and delicious sauce.

Mistereo
Tinoco y Palacios 514, Ruta Independencia

Selva
Macedonio Alcalá 403-Interior 6,
Ruta Independencia

Lechoncito de Oro
Los Libres s/n, Ruta Independencia

For breakfast

Itanoní never disappoints, and I especially like it for breakfast. I'm drawn to anything that comes off the comal, like a tetela (stuffed masa triangles), a memela (crisped, topped masa rounds; see page 42), or one they call "De Ese" with requesón (fresh cheese) and hoja santa (herb), always accompanied by an atole (sweet masa-thickened drink). This restaurant was an early supporter of farmers growing local varieties of corn, beyond blue or white.

Itanoní
Avenida Belisario Domínguez 513,
Oaxaca de Juárez

For a side trip

I always recommend a visit to the **Centro de las Artes de San Agustín**, where the artist Francisco Toledo used to have his workshop, and which is now a cultural center with exhibitions where you can see some of the art he collected. They also have a paper workshop where they work with silkworms and natural pigments. It's a forty-minute drive from Oaxaca, but there are other artisan workshops nearby, and I think it's a great way to get to know Oaxaca. To learn the process of making mezcal, you should also visit a palenque like **Koch**, which has a good hospitality program. Each of these activities is a worthwhile way to spend a morning or afternoon.

Centro de las Artes de San Agustín
Avenida Independencia s/n,
Barrio de Vista Hermosa, San Agustín Etla

Koch
Prol. Emiliano Zapata 1101,
Localidad el Tablón, San Agustín de las Juntas

For dinner

Thalía Barrios's **La Cocina de Humo** feels like a mixture of a Japanese bar and a traditional Oaxacan restaurant. Sit at the counter, where you can see the comal and where the cook serves you by hand. There are stews and always tortillas, but the menu changes weekly or even daily; it's a very beautiful place.

And although it is my own place, I love to eat at **Criollo** and then end the night in the cozy bar with live music and where we have a great selection of mezcals.

La Cocina de Humo
González Ortega 514,
Zona Feb 10 2015, Oaxaca de Juárez

Criollo
Calzada Francisco I. Madero 129,
Oaxaca de Juárez

Where to stay

Hotel Escondido was built by the renowned architect Alberto Kalach. I really like the decor here—the central courtyard is perfect to sit and read or drink a mezcal, and the rooms are very comfortable. I prefer the ones in the new tower, because the ones in the older one tend to have a lot of street noise.

Another hotel is **Casa Criollo**, and what I love about it is exactly what you don't find in other places, like the Turkish bath and the jacuzzi. Usually when you visit Oaxaca, you overindulge in food and drink, and having access to a steam bath always helps to alleviate any discomfort. There's also a great massage service.

Casa Oaxaca (see opposite) is a long-standing boutique hotel, and they offer super-personalized service; they call you by your name. And the breakfast is truly wonderful. Even if I stay at one of the other two places,

I prefer to come here for breakfast. They usually have enfrijoladas (tortillas smothered in bean sauce), enmoladas (mole-drenched tortillas), scrambled eggs, and chilaquiles with mole or with tasajo (dried beef) and amarillito (yellow mole), and the fruit is always spectacular.

Hotel Escondido
Avenida José María Morelos 401, Oaxaca de Juárez

Casa Criollo
Calzada Francisco I. Madero 129, Oaxaca de Juárez

Casa Oaxaca
Constitución 104-A, Oaxaca de Juárez

TRIP 3: Valle de Bravo

by Pati Jinich

Pati Jinich is the author of several cookbooks, including her latest, *Treasures of the Mexican Table*, but she's probably best known as the host of *Pati's Mexican Table*, a PBS cooking show where she highlights the rich and diverse culinary traditions of Mexico through cooking tips, recipes, and stories from her homeland. Her parents once had a small house in Valle de Bravo, a small town two hours from Mexico City, tucked along the shores of Lake Avándaro and known as much for its charm as for its natural beauty. "I love Valle del Bravo because I spent part of my childhood there," says Jinich. "Though my parents no longer have that house, I still go with my family every Christmas holiday." It's a popular weekend destination for chilangos, who flock to the region to relax and unwind. "People might think it's a small place, but around the lake there are many small towns and microclimates," says Jinich. "I love the view of the lake—it gives me peace—and, depending on where you are staying, you can be close to the lake and do lots of water sports like sailing, kayaking, and fishing. My husband and sons love mountain biking, but I love walking and 'pueblear' (visiting small towns or villages)."

For shopping and treats

I like to walk around the town of Valle de Bravo, go to the main square, enter the church, and eat ice cream and ice pops at **Paletería y Nevería La Michoacana**. I'll usually try to visit the market, where, depending on the season, I'll find mushrooms, some giant blackberries that I love, or artichokes grown on nearby farms. Nearby is the **Artisanal Market**, where you can buy textiles woven on a backstrap loom by the Otomí people, and tablecloths, cushions, and napkins made by the Mazahua. There are also many clay items, ideal for cooking things like beans, for example.

Paletería and Nevería
La Michoacana
Calle 5 de Febrero s/n, Centro, Valle de Bravo

Valle de Bravo Artisanal Market
Avenida Benito Juárez Manzana 032,
San Antonio, Centro, Valle de Bravo

For breakfast

The breakfast at **Hotel Rodavento** is as exceptional as the view. I like to order huevos divorciados (eggs with red and green salsa) with cecina. They also have very good quesadillas made with fresh masa, excellent cheese, and other fillings like seasonal mushrooms, huitlacoche (page 56), or squash blossoms. The coffee is also excellent. The spa has just been renovated, and besides the treatments you can also take yoga and meditation classes.

Hotel Rodavento
Carretera Valle de Bravo KM 3.5,
Los Saucos, Valle de Bravo

For something different

In Avándaro, I like the healthy, green, organic vibe of **Alma Tierra Café**. I like to order a green juice, one of the freshly baked breads, and eggs. You can also buy fruit and vegetables that come from their big organic garden, where they practice regenerative agriculture. In the center of Valle de Bravo, there is a classic Mediterranean restaurant called **Dipao** that I have been going to for at least twenty years. I usually order the trout salad, four-cheese artichoke, and spaghetti Parmigiana.

Alma Tierra Café
Rosales, Vega del Llano &, Avandaro,
Valle de Bravo

Dipao
Joaquín Arcadio Pagaza 100,
Centro, Valle de Bravo

For an adventure

Valle de Bravo is one of the most well-known areas in Mexico for paragliding, and **Alas del Hombre** is a company with a lot of experience. I have never done it because I am not into extreme sports, but some people in my family have. Then there's **Pablo's Adventure**, which organizes bike tours and adjusts to each person's experience level. There are options for beginners who enjoy appreciating the landscape, but there are also intermediate routes and adrenaline-packed ones for experts. If there are small children, it's ideal because they actually teach them how to ride a bike. They also provide a light lunch midway through the route for a bit of rest.

Alas del Hombre
www.alas.com.mx

Pablo's Adventure
www.pablosadventure.net

Where to stay

There are two very different places: One is **Hotel Avándaro**, which has a colder mountain climate, and they have just renovated it. It's beautiful with very comfortable rooms, each with a fireplace. I like the fact that you can drive straight to your room because most of them have a garage. For breakfast, I like to order the green chilaquiles with sunny-side-up eggs served in a small pot. They also make quesadillas with fresh masa and a variety of fillings that you can order from the buffet.

There's another hotel that I like, with more of a hipster vibe: **Hotel Cinco Rodavento**, which is in the center of Valle de Bravo. It has a lovely terrace overlooking the lake and the cathedral. The bar is good for cocktails.

Hotel Avándaro
Vega Del Río s/n
Avándaro Subdivision, Valle de Bravo

Hotel Cinco Rodavento
Calle 5 de Mayo 111,
Santa María Ahuacatlán, Valle de Bravo

WHERE TO EAT NEAR MAJOR TOURIST ATTRACTIONS

Many of the city's greatest tourist attractions are in neighborhoods that may not align with the majority of dining and shopping destinations on your list. Instead of grabbing something from the vendors who surround these sites to cater to tourists, here are recommended spots that are particularly close to each destination—all of these restaurants are within a fifteen-minute walk. No one likes a wasted meal.

Arena México
▶ La Docena (page 13)
Avenida Álvaro Obregón 31, colonia Roma Norte

▶ Fideo Gordo (page 100)
Salamanca 87, colonia Roma Norte

Basílica de Santa María de Guadalupe
▶ Lonchería Don Pepe
Montiel 26, colonia Tepeyac Insurgentes, Gustavo A. Madero
The order here is any of the delicious, affordable tortas piled high with meat, cheese, and sweet-hot chipotle chiles.

▶ Pozolería Jalisco (page 152)
Avenida la Fortuna 100, colonia Tepeyac Insurgentes, Gustavo A. Madero

Bosque de Chapultepec (Museo Nacional de Antropología, Castillo de Chapultepec, Museo de Arte Moderno, Museo Tamayo)
▶ El Mirador de Chapultepec (page 15)
Avenida Chapultepec 606, colonia San Miguel Chapultepec

▶ Los Panchos (page <?>)
Tolstoi 9, colonia Anzures

Canales de Xochimilco
▶ Casa Don Neto
Margarita Maza de Juárez 53, colonia San Antonio, Xochimilco
This is a homey charmer with a set lunch menu that includes ample seafood and vegetarian options.

▶ Restaurante Lina Xochimilco
5 de Mayo 82, colonia Xaltocan
Here, enjoy traditional Mexican fare—much of it sourced from Xochimilco's floating gardens—in a restored mansion.

Casa Estudio Luis Barragán
▶ Brutal (page 19)
General Juan Cano 42, colonia San Miguel Chapultepec

▶ Madereros
General Antonio León 72, colonia San Miguel Chapultepec

Monumento a la Revolución Mexicana

► Mesón Puerto Chico (page 65)
José María Iglesias 55, colonia Tabacalera

Museo Anahuacalli

► Cochitlan
Museo 188,
colonia San Pablo Tepetlapa, Coyoacán
The star here is Yucatecan-style lechón al horno, pork braised for fourteen hours.

► Lucrecia (page 109)
Cerrada Simarruba 139b,
colonia Rancho El Rosario, Coyoacán

Museo Casa Estudio Diego Rivera y Frida Kahlo

► Fisher's House
Avenida Altavista 142, colonia San Ángel Inn
This is a high-end concept from a much-loved seafood chain, with brunch dishes daily until one thirty P.M.

► San Ángel Inn (page 110)
Diego Rivera 50, colonia San Ángel Inn

Museo Frida Kahlo

► Los Danzantes (page 108)
Parque Centenario 12, Coyoacán

► Tostadas Coyoacán (page <?>)
Mercado de Coyoacán, Ignacio Allende 49, colonia Del Carmen, Coyoacán

Museo Soumaya

► El Bajío
Avenida Ejército Nacional Mexicano 769, colonia Granada
One of the best spots in Polanco for classic regional dishes is this branch of an influential, long-standing restaurant in an upscale setting.

► Guzina Oaxaca (page 85)
Avenida Presidente Masaryk 513, colonia Polanco

Palacio de Bellas Artes

► Bar La Opera
Avenida 5 de Mayo 10, colonia Centro Histórico

► Ricos Tacos Toluca (page 37)
López 103, Centro Histórico

Plaza de la Constitución (Zócalo)

► Azul Histórico (page 35)
Isabel La Católica 30, Centro Histórico

► Tacos de Canasta El Flaco (page 38)
Calle 5 de Febrero 15-19, Centro Histórico

Plaza Garibaldi

► El Pozole de Moctezuma (page 37)
Moctezuma 12, colonia Guerrero

► Salón Tenampa
Plaza Garibaldi 12, Centro Histórico
Open until three A.M., this cantina is in its one hundredth year (as of 2025) of loud, touristy, boozy fun set to a mariachi soundtrack.

Teotihuacán (Pyramids)

► La Gruta Teotihuacán
Circuito Arqueologico, Avenida del Puente s/n, colonia San Francisco Mazapa
Touristy but stunning, this restaurant in a cave reiterates the ruins' surreal spirit.

ACKNOWLEDGMENTS

Thank you to the entire team—at Eater, on the ground in Mexico City, and beyond—who helped put this book together. The result is a guide full of specific expertise, passion, and know-how that's as exciting and dynamic as the city itself. Thank you to Britt Aboutaleb, Amanda Kludt, and Eric Karp for bringing the Eater guidebook idea to life and to Ellie Krupnick for helping keep us on track. Thank you to Eliane Mancera for the wonderful illustrations and to Nat Belkov and Lille Allen for design collaboration, to Agnieska Spieszny for copy editing, to Lydia Carey for fact checking, and to Stephanie Wu for being a guiding force behind the work from start to finish. Thank you to Hilary Sharp, without whom this series would not exist, and Lindsay Baker and Shyra Smart for ensuring the success of this entire project. And thank you to Aude White and Dane McMillan for making sure people know about everything we do.

Thank you to Laura Dozier, Diane Shaw, Lisa Silverman, and Jenice Kim at Abrams for advising us on how to make the most useful guidebook possible, and for their endless support and patience. Thank you to Natasha Martin, Mamie Sanders, and Danielle Kolodkin at Abrams for their enthusiastic publicity and marketing efforts.

And most importantly, thank you to all the sensational writers, editors, reporters, illustrators, and designers who contributed to Eater's coverage of Mexico City over the years, and most especially Nils Bernstein, who acted as Eater's joyful eyes, ears, and stomach in Mexico City and helped shepherd the local contributors throughout the process. This book would not have been possible without his enthusiasm, nimbleness, collaborative spirit, and devotion to the food and culture of CDMX.

CONTRIBUTORS

Nils Bernstein is a food, drink, and travel writer based in Mexico City. He is the food editor for *Wine Enthusiast* magazine, wrote *The Joy of Oysters*, and has coauthored several cookbooks.

Bill Esparza is a James Beard Award–winning writer, the author of *L.A. Mexicano*, and a frequent guest on food reality television shows as an on-screen personality and fixer.

Raquel del Castillo García has been writing about food for more than fifteen years, with a particular passion for tacos and market stalls around the country. She was the editor of Menu, the food section of the Mexico City newspaper *El Universal*, and is a tour guide for Context Travel.

Natalia de la Rosa is a Mexican food and travel writer, agave spirits collector, and culinary consultant based in Mexico City.

A Mexico City native, **Rulo David** is a writer, editor, DJ, radio host, and TV commentator, covering food, music, sports, politics, and more.

Alonso Ruvalcaba was born and raised in Mexico City. As with most writers, he started by writing poetry and ended up as a freelance food critic. He is a producer on the Amazon Prime series *Pan y Circo* and author of *24 horas de comida en la Ciudad de México*. His next book, *La ciudad de todas las drogas*, is forthcoming.

Liliana López Sorzano is a food and travel writer based between Mexico City and Bogotá, Colombia, where she contributes to local and international media. She is a former editor in chief at *Food & Wine en español*.

Lesley Suter is the award-winning special projects director at Eater and editorial director at Thrillist. Based in Los Angeles, she has spent more than fifteen years covering food, travel, and culture across the globe.

INDEX

Page references in *italics* refer to illustrations.

Editor: Laura Dozier
Designer: Jenice Kim
Managing Editor: Lisa Silverman
Production Manager: Larry Pekarek

Library of Congress Control Number: 2024942515

ISBN: 978-1-4197-6583-4
eISBN: 978-1-64700-891-8

Printed and bound in China
10 9 8 7 6 5 4 3 2 1

Abrams books are available at special discounts when purchased in
quantity for premiums and promotions as well as fundraising or educational
use. Special editions can also be created to specification. For details,
contact specialsales@abramsbooks.com or the address below.

Abrams® is a registered trademark of Harry N. Abrams, Inc.

ABRAMS is represented in the UK and Europe by Abrams & Chronicle Books,
1 West Smithfield, London EC1A 9JU and Média-Participations, 57 rue
Gaston Tessier, 75166 Paris, France.
abramsandchronicle.co.uk and media-participations.com
info@abramsandchronicle.co.uk

ABRAMS The Art of Books
195 Broadway, New York, NY 10007
abramsbooks.com

EATER is a digital media brand dedicated to all things food and dining.
The Eater network comprises a national site covering food and dining
culture, more than twenty city sites tracking local dining scenes, a robust
YouTube channel featuring documentary-style videos about the inner
workings of restaurants, and a variety of social channels, all run by a
diverse team of writers, editors, producers, and contributors. Eater has
been recognized by numerous awards organizations for its achievements
in food journalism and media, including the James Beard Awards, the
American Society of Magazine Editors, and the New York Emmys.

Nils Bernstein is the food editor for *Wine Enthusiast* magazine and
has written and developed recipes for such publications as *Bon Appétit*,
Epicurious, *GQ*, the *New York Times*, *Food & Wine*, and *Men's Journal*.
He is the coauthor of *The Outdoor Kitchen* and *Made in Mexico* and the
author of *The Joy of Oysters*. Bernstein lives in Mexico City. Follow him
on Instagram @nilsbernstein.

Eliane Mancera is an illustrator, multidisciplinary artist, and mother. She has
illustrated for various creative endeavors, including editorial projects, textiles, and
stationery. Born in Mexico City, she now lives in the coastal sage scrub of Tijuana,
where she works, gardens, and hikes. Follow her on Instagram @elyluu.

ATZCA

MIGUEL HIDALGO

CUAJIMALPA

MERCADO MEDELLIN

$10

BENITO JUÁREZ

ALVARO OBREGÓN

MUSEO FRIDA KAHLO

MAGDALENA CONTRERAS

COYOACÁN

TLALPAN